How to

Be a

Living Thing

life

How to

Be a

Living Thing

MEDITATIONS ON INTUITIVE
OYSTERS, HOPEFUL DOVES,
AND BEING HUMAN IN THE WORLD

Mari Andrew

PENGUIN LIFE

VIKING
An imprint of Penguin Random House LLC
1745 Broadway, New York, NY 10019
penguinrandomhouse.com

A Penguin Life Book

VIKING is a registered trademark of Penguin Random House LLC.

Illustrations by the author.

Designed by Cassandra Garruzzo Mueller

LIBRARY OF CONGRESS CONTROL NUMBER: 2025001096

ISBN 9780593831663 (hardcover)
ISBN 9780593831670 (ebook)

Printed in the United States of America
1 3 5 7 9 10 8 6 4 2

The authorized representative in the EU for product safety and compliance is
Penguin Random House Ireland, Morrison Chambers, 32 Nassau Street,
Dublin D02 YH68, Ireland, https://eu-contact.penguin.ie.

For Dan

Contents

AUTHOR'S NOTE

This book is a reflection of the quiet, hidden conversations between us and the natural world—a reminder that our stories, though human, are also animal, earthy, and cosmic. As I ventured through the pages of biology, I marveled at the small and often invisible threads that connect us to the creatures we share this planet with. I've let my imagination wander where science sometimes leaves room for wonder, and in this space, I hope to illuminate some truths that don't always fit neatly into a textbook.

In this book, I've taken certain liberties: blending timelines, reimagining figures, and walking the line between fact and myth. I've woven together history and biology with a thread of whimsy, hoping to echo the beautiful complexity of life itself—sometimes messier, sometimes more wondrous, than primary sources can fully capture. I've played with the spirit of science, where the visible and invisible coexist in a dance of discovery, and where the unknown is just another invitation to wonder.

I hope you'll read this not as a definitive account but as an exploration. An invitation to sit with the animals for a while, to listen deeply and, perhaps, to find something about ourselves reflected in their gaze. We may not understand exactly what they are saying, but we are all part of the same conversation.

Thank you for reading with an open heart!

ON CATS
AND EMBRACING
HUMANNESS

M y cat, Sunny, is so good at being a cat. She's exotic to me: wild, sneaky, and solitary. Her recent ancestors have evolved to get the attention of humans, so she will do charming things like meow in my direction or nibble my hands to wake me up. Most noises scare her, but she proves her inner ferocity when she hunts a fruit fly.

Everything about her is perfectly catlike, and even her most annoyingly catlike moments (jumping up onto a shelf and breaking things) are well within the range of proclivities unique to her species.

I think about this when I remind myself that being good at existing as a human means making mistakes. That missing the mark, flailing around, not knowing what's going on or what I'm doing are well within the range of proclivities unique to my species. *Ah,*

I'm just human-ing! I tell myself, the way I tell myself that Sunny is just *cat-ing* when she scratches my furniture. If I were a beloved pet, I can only imagine my adoring companion saying, *Oh, she's just human-ing. Human-ing today, are we?* And then I'd do something wonderfully, endearingly human, like laugh or have an idea or make a sandwich.

To be human means to be imperfect. But what else does it mean to be human? This question has been on my mind the past few years as my so-called faith in humanity wavers between horror and awe. When I read about what we do with our enormous capacity for violence, I nearly convince myself that our species must have resulted from some destructive glitch in an otherwise harmonious universe. Moments later when I see evidence of our enormous capacity for compassion, I return to my long-held belief that people must be good at heart.

You see, humans are my favorite animal.

And that's saying a lot, because I love all animals very much. Yes, even rats, but we'll get to that later.

What's not to love about humans? We are an ever-evolving species known for our inventiveness, silliness, sociability, and staggering range of emotions, which we channel to create murals on the sides of structures we built and songs on instruments we invented.

Oh right—there's a lot not to love about humans! As of right now, around the world there are multiple vicious conflicts going on in which people are justifying doing unspeakable things to other people. I see images and read reports from these wars that chill me to the bone. I read reports from my own city that are just as horrifying: abuse, exploitation, vandalization of a food pantry, destruction of a wildlife habitat, and exploitation of beings and resources.

When I share my love of animals with others, I often hear the same response: "I love animals too! I love them more than humans. Humans suck." And I very much get that sentiment—give me a groundhog over most people any day. But I really love humans too! I don't believe we suck. It's only when I get caught in the question "Are we good or bad?" that I doubt my belief in us.

The capricious relationship we have to our own kind is probably as old as we are: war, romance, sacrifice, cruelty, and friendship have always existed and have always hardened or softened our connection to those around us.

Who could blame us for confusion about our own species? Our behavior is contradictory: The same people who advanced lyrical poetry also gleefully fed their citizens to lions and cheered from the seats of the Colosseum. The same men who were brilliant and brave enough to create a template for representative democracy weren't wholehearted enough to exclude the brutality of slavery from it.

One of the most evildoing figures in history was an animal advocate and landscape painter, and some of our most lionized figures in the arts and politics were abusive lovers and awful parents. Those of us who follow feel-good social media accounts just to swoon at the kind deeds of our fellow humans may also binge true crime stories to indulge in the dark reality that we are all capable of so much worse.

As one of the most human-loving poets, Walt Whitman, wrote, we contain multitudes, yet we seem to have a lot of trouble accepting contradictions in one another. It doesn't cause us nearly as much grief to acknowledge that bears are beautiful and ferocious. Or to admit that the pets we adore are often the bane of our existence. That's why, the less time I spend unraveling the good/bad binary and the more time I spend in and with the natural world, the more I feel love for all of us humans—even myself.

If I were going with a binary, Sunny is not a *good* cat. Not by pet-owning standards anyway. She's too feral for lap sitting and too dependent to be on her own for long. Needy *and* avoidant is a tough combo (and probably one that many who have spent years dating are cautious of). That's perhaps why she was in the shelter for a long time.

Yet I wouldn't change a thing about her. I get a thrill watching my cat skeptically accept small portions of the love I have for her, and I appreciate that it takes her a long time to trust for reasons I'll never know. She wholly gives what she can when she's ready, and every little nudge or mew in my direction is worth celebrating.

Sunny's default nature is so nervous that even the smallest display of affection is a triumph of her trust in me. A simple brush against my leg is all she can offer most days, and because it took years to get there, it means the world to me.

I adopted Sunny at the city shelter from a list of animals to be euthanized that same week I got her. Trust issues aside, her very existence is a miracle of timing. Every day she lives is a cosmic bonus, so every one of her acts of connection is a bonus too.

My cat is so easy to love, not because she cuddles (she doesn't) or comes when I call (not a chance) or lets me kiss her on the nose (my greatest dream, never to come true). She's easy to love because she gives what she can in the time that she has, and I consider that small gift to be hugely valuable.

She reminds me that you can fail every day and still be loved beyond your wildest dreams. She shows me what it looks like to be cared for without a single condition. She looks grace right in the face and hisses at it, and yet she is precious. As a living thing, she does what her species of living things has done forever.

For time immemorial, philosophers, writers, artists, and scientists have defined humans by the ways we are *unlike* animals. That is to say, what makes us human is what differentiates us from animals.

Not only is this bad biology—we don't define a goldfish by how it differs from a rosebush—it has gotten us into all kinds of dangerous pickles throughout time. If the public believes that humans are by definition not like animals, then when a person exhibits any trait that could be considered "animal-esque," it puts that person in danger of being regarded as less-than-human. When societies sever themselves from the natural world, the humans with the most "natural" tendencies (giving birth, for example) are treated with less respect.

Our planet also suffers when we define humans as "not animals." Though animal scientists have proven over and over that mammals feel love for their young and birds feel grief for their dead and rats feel regret and ponies feel empathy, all of this research can easily be dismissed with, "It's just instinct." By this logic, the mournful cries that dairy cows wail when their babies are repeatedly taken from them immediately after birth are "just instinctual," and it's simply instinct when they desperately try to hide their babies from people the next time they're born.

Isn't there a possibility that all animal behavior—including that of humans—is both instinctual for the purpose of our species, survival *and* tied to real heartbreak, love, and joy?

So, here's my idea: Why don't we try seeing ourselves in animals in order to find out more about who we are? How about instead of focusing on how much we *differ* from animals, we look to them for some much-needed universal truths about ourselves so we can relate to one another better?

If we can shift characterizing humans as "not animals" to "a beautifully imperfect species whose very definition allows for our pain and our failures," then perhaps we can set ourselves up for more compassion. Sunny has certainly taught me a lot about that.

Cats are one of the last animals to be domesticated by humans, so they don't have as many adaptations toward us as dogs or horses do. Even the cuddliest and most trainable kitties still have rebellious tendencies and unpredictable moods—remnants from a recent (relatively speaking) past when they had nothing to do with people.

They are still tightly connected to their untamed animal-ness, which makes them imperfect pets but excellent teachers. While Sunny hasn't evolved to automatically make me feel great about myself when I enter the door (most days, she couldn't care less), she also hasn't evolved to let me almost forget that she's an autonomous being. And because of her stubborn insistence on living as an autonomous being, she reminds me that I'm one too.

Like Sunny, I exist in a body, but unlike her, I'm preoccupied with my body's appearance. Sunny seems only interested in doing a simple survey for how she feels in her body on a given day: *Am I in pain? Am I hungry? Am I tired? Am I thirsty?* Then she acts accordingly. I neglect my bodily cues and nitpick wrinkles—those normal signs of life—instead.

Like her, I have desires and wishes, but unlike Sunny, the thrill of chasing after them isn't satisfying enough for me. Sunny probably doesn't feel like a loser if she doesn't grasp the spider or laser-pointer beam in her paws the way I do when I face rejection. She merely exerted some energy and now she'll either nap or try again. Meanwhile, I stew in inadequacy.

Like her, I'm intuitive and perceptive, but unlike Sunny, I override my own intuition with society-constructed logic like "But this is what we've always done" or "You're too sensitive." If we shared a spoken language, I would *never* tell Sunny she was too sensitive; I trust that her reactions are in proportion to the wounds of her past or her feline instinct. Yet I judge myself for being anxious, cautious, or hurt over a seemingly minor infliction. *I'm so high-maintenance*, I chastise myself. I tell myself I need to be *easier* for others, meaning less emotional—something I'd never expect of my cat, because I understand that she's a living creature and not an iPad.

Reminding myself that I am a living thing, a body with needs and feelings and fears every bit as real as the ones Sunny shows me, has profoundly shifted the way I see myself and other humans. Sunny's living-thing-ness is what I believe gives her inherent worth, lovability, and the right to her own way of being in the world.

In these pages, my hope is that by reflecting a little more on your living-thing-ness, you will embrace your own experience of being a learning, growing, squishy, inconsistent, imperfect, alive creature, part of a species that can be confusing sometimes, in a world that can be confusing sometimes. And I hope that you too can fall in love with the creatures of the world as much as I've fallen in love with my own feisty, unruly, hissy senior tabby.

How to

Be a

Living Thing

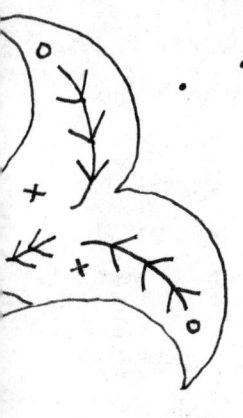

Chapter 1

ON ORCAS
AND THE PRIVILEGE
OF STRIVING

My favorite game to play as a kid was called Town. It was the perfect activity for an only child because I could play it alone for hours and hours. Basically, it involved writing a list of townsfolk (the more elaborately named, the better) and drawing a map of their town. I would label each house with the people who lived there and what they did for work or where they went to school. Then I'd draw the doctor's office, the bakery, the gas station, and all the other places where adults went during the day.

Surely I was heavily inspired by the genre of movie that opens with a lively description of its setting and all the jobs for the people there, like Belle's "Little town, full of little people" in *Beauty and the Beast*, or the more crass version, "Good Morning Baltimore" in *Hairspray*, which introduces the neighborhood flasher and the local bar bum. In *Fiddler on the Roof*'s opening number "Tradition," Tevye lists the responsibilities of the four types of people in his town of Anatevka: the mamas, the papas, the daughters, the sons. The eponymous song of *In the Heights* gives the who's who in the barrio as workers from the salon and cab company dance into the local bodega for coffee.

As a child I found this orderly activity of the adult world to be comforting. "When I grow up, I will have a job, and I will go to it, and these are the people I will meet throughout the day." All the lined notebooks I filled with my various towns spoke to a pleasant busyness that I imagined awaited me in my future: things to do, people to see, places to go.

Maybe I was indoctrinated by places in children's books like Richard Scarry's Busytown, but I never daydreamed about leisure in my future. Rather, I envisioned bustling mornings and weekend errands. I admired the high-heeled career woman, always on her way to some appointment or event and getting there just in time, hair windswept and nails shining. I strove for action.

Now, as an adult woman with a career, when I'm rushing from one thing to the next, hair more wild than windswept, bumping into my fellow townsfolk, I dream of being stuck on an island with nothing to do and no other humans in sight. All this rushing around and brushing against strangers gets annoying. How inconvenient to have to actually *deal* with people as opposed to drawing them on a map or watching them cheerfully sing their introductions in a movie.

And how tedious at times to actually have to go out and run errands, get groceries, make appointments. Unlike the patrons of

In the Heights' colorful bodega, I am not always sashaying and spinning my way to procure cleaning supplies. And the shop owners are not always as helpful as they are in Busytown.

A lot of real life, come to find out, is challenging! Not smooth sailing like the bump-free buses full of cooperative commuters singing out "Good morning Baltimore!"

Countless start-up inventors are constantly scheming to identify the "pains" of real life—doing chores, preparing food, and so on—and figuring out ways to help us avoid those pains. Some of these inventions have really taken off, like food-delivery sites to relieve you of the horror of having to make a phone call. And some of them failed immediately, like an app intended to make restaurant dining a breeze: you reserve, order, and pay all on your phone and never even have to so much as glance at a waiter.

In the early days of lockdown during the first wave of Covid-19, there were a ton of new ideas, an intense blossoming of mass conveniences. Hoity-toity restaurants that once prohibited takeout now offered a range of ways to "Have the hoity-toity experience at home!" (in so many words). Symphonies and ballets, once inaccessible to many of us, started streaming performances to the comfort of your living room. Galleries gave virtual tours of their art collections, advertising that no one would be able to block your view. If you had a screen, you had a way to "attend" live performances, eat "at" good restaurants, "visit" museums.

The quotation marks are doing a lot of work here, because, as it turns out, none of it felt real. Humans can't be tricked into believing they're at an opera house when they're really eating Doritos on a beanbag chair, nor does a forty-dollar pork chop have much panache when it slides out of a take-out container onto your IKEA plate. There were many moments during lockdown when I would have sworn off screens for life if it meant that I could be bothered by someone blocking my view at a museum. I *prayed* to be bothered.

I missed having to get up from my seat at the theater to let someone into the row only to then have to listen to them chomping on nuts through the whole performance. I missed squeezing onto a subway train and breathing in the gym-sock-and-heavy-perfume-combo smell. I missed forcing small talk with a chatty waiter and walking a few blocks out of my way to pick up cleaning supplies. In a bizarre twist, it was almost as though life had gotten *too* convenient. I didn't want the museum to come to me. I wanted to go to it. And I would have sat in traffic and stood in line to do that.

During the lockdown, I read an article about orca whales by Lori Marino, president of the Whale Sanctuary Project. I've always had a soft spot for orcas, having grown up in Seattle. In school we learned the local Indigenous legends about the orcas, how the "blackfish" became both killers and protectors and now guard the sea. Depictions of them jumping into the air grace postcards and picture books about the Pacific Northwest. Who wouldn't be enchanted by the sight of one leaping straight up from the water with the power and grace of a prima ballerina?

I suppose that was the idea when people started capturing orcas from the ocean and training them for shows where they performed their signature leaps for wide-eyed, cheering crowds a few times a day. Despite their reputation as killers, orcas have always gotten along well with humans and apparently were quick and easy to train for these shows. They would spin, shimmy, and soar on command, delighting families at marine parks all over the world.

Seemingly very low maintenance, the whales appeared happy to do their routines for the reward of fish, then go back to swimming around their pools until the next show. The trainers at SeaWorld and its competitors told audiences that orcas were much safer and happier in marine facilities than in the wild. After all, there was a zero percent chance that whales would ever go hungry or face danger in their pools. They were fed fish all day and faced no challenges apart from an easy routine.

But Lori Marino's article told a different story of whales in captivity. In tanks, where some orcas aren't provided so much as a toy to play with, whales are understimulated to the point of life-threatening stress. They've been known to self-mutilate after years in a swimming pool, banging their heads on the walls or even attempting to jump out in an apparent effort to die. It's as though their captive existence feels so egregiously wrong that it's painful and not even worth living.

Why would such an easy life cause them to suffer? In the ocean, orcas are met with all kinds of toils and troubles: the hunt for food, problems within the pod, parasites, and predators. You'd think the swimming pool would be like a lifelong spa day in comparison!

In her article, Lori Marino pointed out that whales evolved over millennia for the *ocean*—not for a swimming pool. Both situations involve water, sure, but that's like comparing sitting on an airplane to hiking across a mountain range because they're both up high. Orcas' intuition, intelligence, and bodies are intricately suited to a complex, ever-changing environment. So when they live in a display tank with highly artificial circumstances, they don't feel safe and stress-free; they feel constant anxiety.

As I read this from the chair where I'd been attending virtual baby showers, ordering delivery gnocchi, and taking online history classes to pass those bleak hours at home, I realized that all this confinement activity was actually causing anxiety. Apart from, you know, the regular pandemic anxiety.

Turns out that pandemic Zoom happy hours got really old, really fast. There was a highly artificial veneer to the super-sterile existence of seeing other humans only through a screen, as though I could have "people on demand." It wasn't supposed to be this way. It felt wrong; so wrong that I'd get a little nauseated every time a new invitation for a virtual gathering popped up.

Back to the whale world. Marino writes that proponents of marine parks will point to the leviathans circling around a pool and argue, "Look! They're stress-free! Imagine if they were out there fighting off predators and looking for fish—they're living a life of luxury with daily feedings straight into their mouths!" Getting a sufficient supply of food with nothing to do but perform repetitive tricks might not be demanding, but the chronic boredom of an "easy life" with little stimulation and no challenges is absolutely stressful.

I can see why marine-park enthusiasts got to that justification, although as a member of the *Free Willy* generation, it's obvious to me that orcas will develop all sorts of physical and mental problems from living in a tank. But I hadn't factored in the stressfulness, even torture, of so-called *ease*. It wasn't until I looked around at my deliveries and my calendar items for the day—none of which required me to move my tush off the chair for one moment—that I got a small sense of what exactly Marino was talking about. *Yikes*, I thought. *Set those whales free!*

Of course, lockdown is an extreme example of how a sanitized existence is a unique type of hellishness. But I wonder if there are other, more subtle ways that we are keeping ourselves in a proverbial swimming pool, left to swim in circles, questioning why it's not making us happy.

My friend Ada intensely wanted to find her soulmate throughout her entire twenties. She wasn't constantly dating, but she sure was constantly longing. She described it as a physical ache, the ghost pain of something missing. Meanwhile, she traveled, explored, made good friends, and took interesting jobs. The whole time, she yearned for romantic partnership.

Eventually she found him, and it was wonderful, and the wedding was beautiful. Everything she wanted. She adores her husband and they love being together, but a month into her marriage she noticed a low-level ennui that started following her around. What *was* that stubborn pebble of depression in her shoe? It didn't make sense.

After some honest thought, she figured it out: for two decades, Ada had been keeping her eyes and heart open for the love of her life at all times. Every day held possibility: *Is today the day? Is he the one?* Every vacation, every invitation was an opportunity to meet her soulmate. He could come around any corner, open any door. Her strong desire, however frustrating, was also tremendously motivating, and often exciting.

Postwedding, she realized that a little fire within her had been extinguished. While the flame of hope sometimes burned her, she missed it when it was gone, and it took some time to grieve that loss before she could fully embrace her new chapter.

Likewise, if I'm honest with myself about when I'm happiest, it's when I'm actively complaining about work! A finished product might give me a five-second smile, but work is a consistent thrill. The unpredictability of it is exciting enough, but the toughness makes me feel big and alive. I feel like I'm fully human-ing when I'm striving toward an accomplishment, on the edge of my seat as to whether I'm actually going to make it.

If you could take a pill and suddenly have your strongest possible body without lifting weights, would you? If you could pay to be carried up Mount Everest and be placed on top for a photo op, would you? If you could snap your fingers and skip having to learn piano and go right to Carnegie Hall, would you? There might be some work that we'd be happy to skip, but I bet you can see how working toward a goal, however challenging, could be more joy-giving than a magic snap of the fingers.

There's a funny theory from psychoanalyst Jacques Lacan about the human drive to strive for things. Lacan called it "objet petit a," or "object a." The "a" stands for anything we desire, and the idea is that as soon as we get it, we'll replace it with something else. Lacan believed that we always need something to desire, so much so that we will get in our own way because we subconsciously don't actually want it. We intuitively know that getting what we want will *not* make us happy, and we'd rather not deal with that absurd reality!

Convenience doesn't give us joy, and, strangely enough, neither does satisfaction. In the human mind, a little pocket of dissatisfaction goes a long way. Without it, there's no striving, and striving seems to be a big part of human happiness.

When I think back to all those glorious opening scenes of movies where the setting is introduced through jubilant song, I realize now that the narrator wasn't giving us a tour in order to show us how the town worked. Instead, they were showing us what was all about to change. Orderliness and predictability are comforting concepts, but they don't captivate our imaginations the way that challenges do. Great movies are stories about how the world isn't as tidy as we had hoped, but it's so much better that way. Hearts expand, minds transform, and by the end, the setting is different.

The town doesn't run as smoothly, but, as Oliver Burkeman wrote in "Escaping the Efficiency Trap—and Finding Some Peace of Mind," his 2021 critique of efficiency for *The Wall Street Journal*, "Smoothness, it turns out, is a dubious virtue, since it's often the unsmoothed textures of life that make it livable, helping to nurture the relationships that are crucial for mental and physical health, and for the resilience of our communities."

Day-to-day difficulties are the residue of what gives us the most joy: being fully in the world with other humans. Not via screen, not only with a drive-by delivery person, but out in all those fabulous inconvenient textures and a complex, free-ranging sociocultural milieu.

Whenever I played Town, the final step was to begin creating dramatic problems for the citizens who lived there and figuring out how to solve them—the fun of any imaginative simulation. I had countless variations of civic obstacles to mimic: where to make room for a new skateboard park, how to deal with a bad guy for a mayor, what to choose for the community theater's next musical.

As a child, I intuitively sought out problems to solve and goals to strive for, even through the avatars of my stick-figure townspeople, my pioneers, my dolls. In *The Oregon Trail*, the computer game that took hours and hours off my youth, I held my breath while my pioneering fake family forged the river in one piece.

My friends and I improvised scenarios where our American Girl dolls were in an argument, and we'd speak for them in old-timey mid-Atlantic accents to work through it.

Somewhere between schoolyard challenges of pretend games and adulthood with its higher-stakes responsibilities, I forgot that *not having what I wanted* was a good thing. A potentially fun thing. And, with the sensory-deprived captive orcas in mind, a privilege. Many animals and humans, for one reason or another, don't *get* to navigate the vast outside world with its various unpredictabilities and surprises, and I realized that really *wanting* something was a gift. A key to happiness, perhaps.

Like my Town-playing self, children tend to be so much more connected to their animal instincts than adults. When you ask a kid what they want to do when they grow up, none of them answer "Stay home all day" the way a forty-six-year-old might. They list occupations that require action and engagement with the world—astronaut, doctor, Olympic athlete, scientist. They know that satisfaction in life doesn't come from doing nothing but from doing *something*—many somethings, and great somethings that take work and sacrifice and grit.

Meanwhile, adults like me scan for what we don't already have and resent the gap between where we are now and what we want. Adults have come up with all kinds of ways to make life more efficient and, in the process, prevent any discomfort that may lead to astonishment. I know I've come back home from a day at the aquarium, shaking my head with pity for the wild animals confined to spaces that surely vex them—if only they could join their family for a hunt!—only to order some paper towels online when they're available at the family-run market down the street. I forget that the difficulty in *pursuing what I want* isn't a burden but a human birthright.

How often do I want more for whales than I demand for myself: complexity, variability, risks, and challenges that come with being alive in a miraculous world?

Perhaps the answer lies somewhere in G. K. Chesterton's melancholy quote: "The world will never starve for want of wonders;

but only for want of wonder." If we want to experience life as one of those breathtaking blackfish who take flight above the ocean's surface only to splash back down into a sea full of tests and treasures, we've got to give up on ease. Longing and striving are essential to our species' joy, and we begin to hold our own selves captive when we exchange them for convenience.

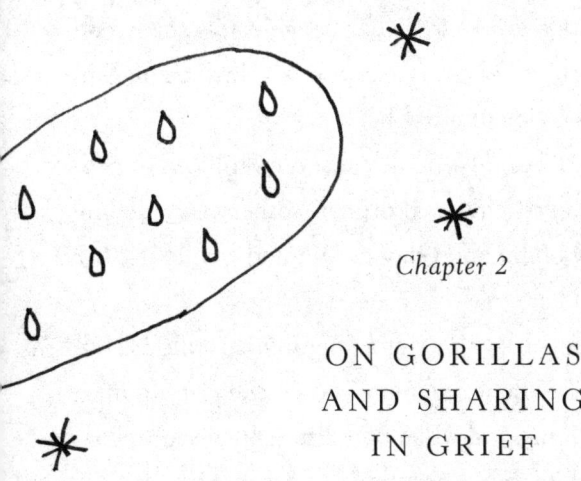

Chapter 2

ON GORILLAS
AND SHARING
IN GRIEF

One of the most iconic *National Geographic* covers features a tiny tabby, doing nothing out of the ordinary for a kitten. She's simply being cuddled, and seemingly enjoying herself. The remarkable aspect of the picture is who's cuddling her: a 280-pound western lowland gorilla named Koko.

When the photo ran, people were already fascinated with Koko. Born at the San Francisco Zoo, Koko began learning sign language at the age of one from her trainer, Dr. Penny Patterson. Koko quickly became a prodigy. She mastered the signs, inventing her own complex combinations of words. She told jokes, relayed memories, and expressed her imagination via signs.

When Koko asked for a pet cat, rejecting a stuffed animal in favor of the real deal, the public was captivated. Koko treated All

Ball, her tailless abandoned kitten, as her baby. Just as she would be with a gorilla offspring, Koko was exceptionally loving and gentle with All Ball, even trying to nurse her.

When the *National Geographic* issue came out, millions of people were amazed by Koko. This wild primate, otherwise crawling around and munching on bamboo shoots, adopted a child not her own and lovingly held her.

I get the amazement. I love to watch any interspecific friendship unfold on YouTube. Be it a donkey and chicken or a guinea pig and terrier, I find it magical when two different species recognize something shared in each other.

But being amazed and being connected are two different things. We may be in awe of a gorilla who learns sign language and keeps a pet, but it wasn't until Koko began grieving that we could see *ourselves* in her.

One day, when All Ball was still a kitten, she wandered away from Koko's enclosure and was killed by a car. Penny sat down with the gorilla and signed the news: "All Ball was hit by a car." Koko had lived a sheltered life, away from the dangers of poaching and other threats to gorillas in the wild. Yet still she understood the permanence of death right away. In response to the terrible news, Koko signed, "Bad, sad, bad" and "Frown, cry, frown, sad, trouble."

Critics of the gorilla's communicative abilities suggested Koko was only responding to those around her rather than expressing her own thoughts. Maybe she was signing "frown" because her trainer was frowning.

I was around five when I looked around my kindergarten classroom and thought about how I'd never really know if the color blue I was seeing matched the blue that others were seeing. How would I know if "sad" was the same for them as it was for me, or if "hard" homework wasn't as hard for them? Words seemed so flimsy all of a sudden.

For Koko, all we have to go on about her grieving state is "Bad, sad, bad." But to be fair, this is all we have to go on even when we're talking to another person. To communicate through words or signs, we have to trust that our definitions match up. For a teenager who isn't particularly verbose, or a gorilla for that matter, words may feel frustrating in their limitations.

Later that night, after signing her feelings in response to the news, Koko's keepers heard her begin to cry. It was a distinct cry she hadn't let out since she was a baby left alone in her cage at night: a hooting sound that could be heard from across the zoo. Penny called it a cry that means "someone's leaving me." Koko bellowed, roared, and pounded on her cage walls all night.

If you've ever suffered a loss, in those tender early days when words are useless for expressing sorrow, you know that "How are you feeling?" is impossible to answer. The only expression that will do is a sound. For Koko, it was a mournful hooting. For me, it's tears and whimpering. Words can be slippery, open to interpretation.

But a cry, we understand with our belly.

I once read an essay written by the father of a college girl who was hit by a truck and killed while biking home from her job near my apartment. The father wrote five pages of memories of his daughter, from the time she was a baby up until the day she died, and he concluded by lamenting that he was not able to stand in front of the truck and protect her.

"I ache," he wrote, "I howl."

When I read those words, I thought of a nature show I watched about elephants. The show claimed that elephants experience powerful emotions, which are most evident when they are in mourning. In one instance, after an elephant was killed by poachers, the rest of the herd immediately gathered around the body in a large circle. Then they started stomping their feet and crying. Their cries were enormous and lingering, a unified sobbing like the collective howl of wolves. It didn't sound like any noise I'd expected could come from an elephant; it was so loud and terrible and sad.

Animal scientists are constantly researching ways that different species can communicate with one another. Perhaps the only shared language that we can fully trust is the language of pain. Words are subjective. A howl is not.

The first and last time I used a mousetrap, at the behest of my Manhattan landlord, the contraption failed as they so often do. The injured mouse dragged itself under the fridge, inaccessible to me, and I listened to it wail all night. I cried too, hating that I'd inflicted so much pain on a critter who was just trying to find warmth in this harsh world. I tried to console myself. "Maybe the mouse's cry is just shock, and maybe the shock has numbed the pain." But that's not how it works for us, for gorillas, for elephants, for mice.

Pain is pain is pain, and we recognize the sound of it from any species. I wonder if all the crying species developed this unmistakable type of vocalization in order to ask one another for help, a sort of interspecies language. I may not know what my cat wants when she circles my legs, meowing even after being fed, but I sure as hell knew what her scream meant when I touched her stomach and realized she was sick. "I'm so sorry," I told her, and hoped the language of sympathy was also recognizable between species.

It's inevitable living in a big city that you will see a stranger crying here and there. I've been that stranger to many, eliciting a range of responses. After a day of bureaucratic frustrations and homesickness while working abroad in Chile, I sobbed into my fists on the taxi ride home. Over and over, the driver repeated "*Pobrecita*," poor thing. *Pobrecita, pobrecita, pobrecita.* In New York, I've been hugged and offered tissues by passersby, and most other times I've been respectfully ignored—sometimes with a subtle knowing nod.

It's embarrassing, I guess, but I've never felt overly self-conscious about it. When I see a stranger crying, whether on a plane or across the café table from a presumed partner, I understand with my belly. *I've been you before and I'll be you again*, I try to silently communicate.

Maybe a gift in witnessing one another cry is that we are reminded how many times our own hearts have been scarred and torn, and somehow we made it through the day, then the next day, and as many days as it took to be here—to be the person no longer crying.

There's no way to verbally say that to a grieving gorilla. There's no way to explain to her in words or even signs that someday it's going to be okay, that in a few years she'll actually find that her love is big enough to cradle another kitten, this time with orange fur. That's spoken encouragement, expressed from the mind. In her acute agony, Koko expressed from her belly those same hooting cries she let out as an infant before she learned her first sign.

What Koko taught the human world through her crying is that pain is unmistakable. Even *National Geographic* may not have totally understood what was going on in Koko's brain when she cradled a tailless kitten, but everyone can understand what was going through her brain, and heart and soul and belly, when she sobbed over her loss. To love is something of a miracle (especially between gorilla and kitten), but to ache is inevitable.

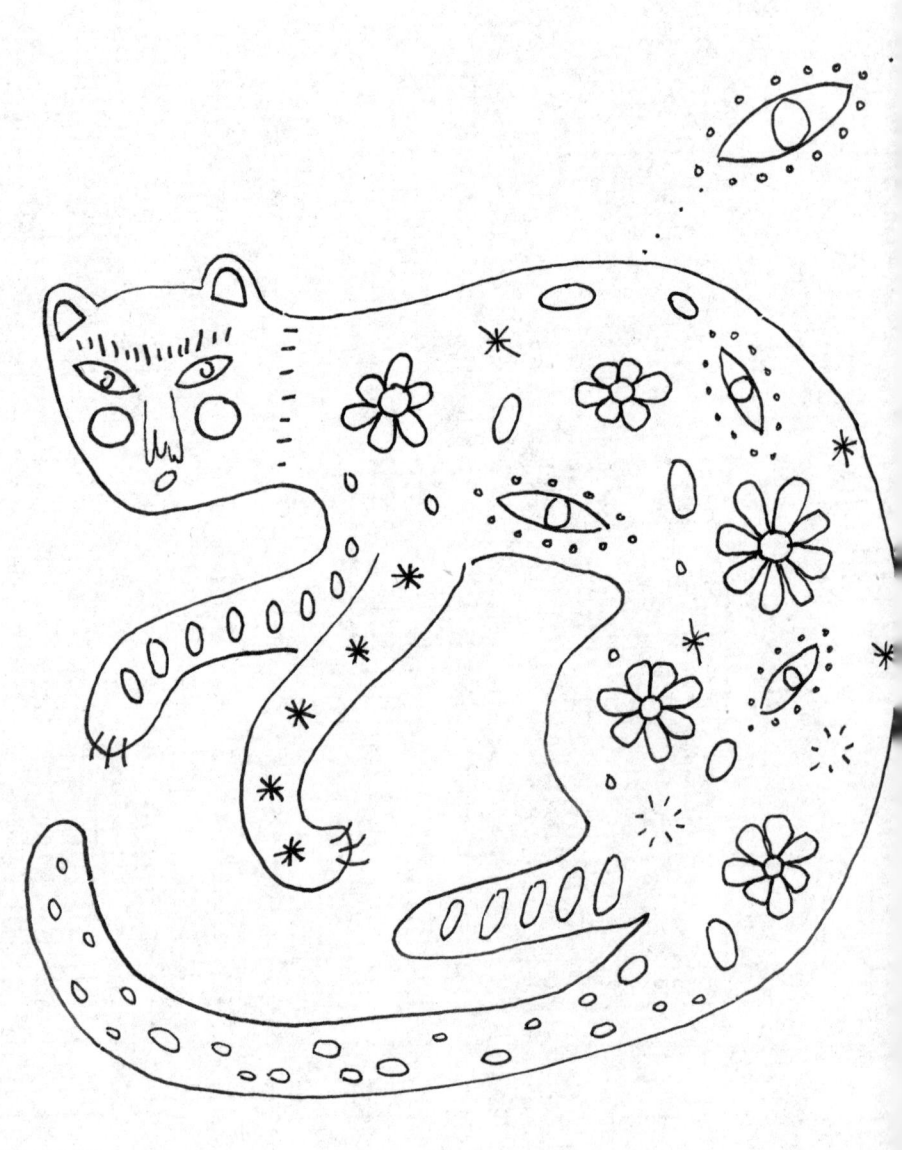

Chapter 3

ON PANTHERS
AND PAYING
CLOSER ATTENTION

My senior cat, Sunny, often startles me when she revisits the huntress tendencies of her youth. She sleeps about twenty-three hours a day, but every now and then she'll gather a wealth of energy from an unknown source and slither around my apartment like she's a killer with a litter of cubs to feed. Because my apartment is free of rodents and roaches, she often has to make do with a rubber band or slice of ribbon left on the floor.

Today, it's a sock.

Amused, I watch her as she zeroes in.

Her entire tiny body morphs into a weapon, both arrow and bow, as she crouches down and pulls back her elbows so she's ready to shoot herself forward. Her eyes become calculators as she concocts a game plan for the attack; not even the siren song of a can opener can seduce her from the hunt.

And then she shoots, she scores.

She captures the sock with two paws and rips into it with her teeth. Within seconds, she's over it, and walks toward dinner.

I can only imagine how much energy she just exerted, literally throwing her entire body into one singular pursuit. No wonder she goes back to sleep for the day.

In the mornings, I walk through Prospect Park. It is all manicured wilderness—there is no natural danger here. My hairdresser shared a fun New York rumor that Frederick Law Olmsted, who codesigned both Central Park and Prospect Park, consulted his wife to configure the shapes of the walking paths to the intuitive movement of the body. She was a dancer and had direct access to the kind of forgotten knowledge that the rest of us need books and retreats to figure out: how to move naturally through the world.

Whether or not the rumor is true, I often close my eyes and let my body instinctively guide me around the park, observing if I really do want to swerve left here or spiral over there. And I always conclude: Mrs. Olmsted was right! These paths do reflect my human body's innate proclivities.

But soon enough, I tire of trying to find peace and connectedness in the urban wild, and I take out my phone.

At once, my whole being is consumed. My shoulders scrunch and my eyes become calculators, laser beams, headlights. On one screen, I get an email reminding me that a project is past due. I frantically type back, "Will do!" Fear heats my entire body.

I numb my nagging worry by scrolling through Instagram Stories. In one frame, a link to donate. The next, an acquaintance squint-smiling under what appears to be the Mediterranean sun, judging by the Sanpellegrino and Aperol bottles in the background. I click through her vacation, which includes a subtle reference to her new boyfriend who I investigate for at least a minute. Then more sites to donate to, articles to read, accounts to follow in order to educate myself. Oh right, the wildfire. The war. The twelve-day yoga challenge. The link to preorder, the link to register now, the link to scarves on sale, the link to the ceramic bowls in the foreground of a celebrity's kitchen feature in the newest issue of an Italian home magazine.

In less than a minute, I have just experienced twenty-five unprocessed emotions—I'm jealous, judgmental, upset, excited, insecure, arrogant, helpless, guilty, and suddenly noticing a gaping hollowness in my soul because I don't own those ceramic bowls.

I have gone through all of these emotions with the same intense focus my cat uses when hunting socks.

Studies show that we will focus on our email and social media as though they are something we're hunting. Our entire body will zero in on what's on the screen, to the point where we ignore our actual, living surroundings. Though we don't tend to get attacked in the wilderness as much as our ancestors, our evolutionary tools to scan for danger are still active and have translated to screens: focusing on a comment from someone we don't know or the boss messaging for a private meeting. Our heartbeat quickens; our fear heightens. Those emails about an overdue project evoke an ancient panic about being rejected from the tribe. Yikes!

Because our whole nervous system attunes itself to a screen, our bodies believe that what's on the screen is more important than what's happening outside. When I'm hunched over my phone, even half watching a video that a friend just sent the group chat, an actual human who taps me on the shoulder to ask for directions can startle the living daylights out of me. Our bodies really, truly believe that what's going on in the phone is as significant as an ancient hunt or a prehistoric danger, and that it requires rapt focus with every cell of our being.

Perhaps this is why the news has begun to feel more real than our real lives: because it exists in a screen designed to steal our full-body attention.

Both my dainty cat Sunny of my Brooklyn apartment and the majestic black panther of the South Asian rainforests belong to the Felidae family, the most highly developed carnivorous hunters of all the mammals.

Though Sunny probably wouldn't last too long in the rainforest without her cans of pâté and heated bed, her physicality is impressively panther-like, and I can easily see the resemblance to her fierce wild cousin.

Panthers too spend a good amount of time sleeping (albeit with no heated beds). They exert unfathomable energy when they go in for the kill, so they rest up and spend time in cautious attentiveness to make sure that their hunt will be worth the internal storm they summon when they charge on their prey.

They stalk the object of their desire slowly. They observe its behavior and track its movements with the vigilance of a detective. From a couple of moments to a few hours, the panther assesses when it will pounce, how it will attack, and how much energy it will use from its limited but potent reserve.

Early humans didn't have nearly the muscle power or speed of a big cat, but they too had to conserve and mindfully distribute their attention during a scavenge or a hunt. Procuring food took a *lot* out of them (braving the grocery store ahead of Thanksgiving doesn't hold a candle!), and they couldn't waste precious energy climbing trees with too few berries or running after a critter who was just too fast. Ancient (and even fairly recent!) humans knew that attention is a limited resource.

Now we give it away all over the place. Or, rather, it is constantly taken from us. No wonder I can hardly stay engrossed through a two-hour movie.

As I scroll through my phone, I see a pajama ad, then an Instagram story that tells me, in red text, "If you have a friend or family member who voted YES, don't talk to them." I think of my soulful cousin, who voted differently from me but would never hesitate to help a vulnerable neighbor in need.

My body is hunched in full focus toward my phone. For a few moments, I'm preoccupied with questions while straining to be obedient: If I really believe in my values, should I cut off communication? Am I out of integrity when I skip political discussions with my cousin and ask about his pets and woodworking projects instead?

It's only the next morning when I return to the forest, phone off and eyes following a cardinal wandering from tree to tree, that I begin reconsidering that Instagram story with the red text, this time with a relaxed nervous system.

That Instagram story will never know the relative who taught the little ones to skip stones at the pond that looks like a sheet of cobalt under the twilight sky at nine p.m. on a summer's night, when fireflies were mistaken for porch lights. It will never know how that same family member remembers to save Grandma the last slice of peach pie. That Instagram story doesn't know how he was shot in the hand two summers later, and afterward journeyed through hell on earth to break free from drug use. How he's struggling to raise a daughter alone and often succumbs to self-worthlessness.

Is abandonment the answer? Will withdrawing my presence be enough to change his mind during the next election? And if so, will I share what happened on Instagram, a frame on a story that will be forgotten one moment later?

I'm hyperfixated on dangers that only live in one app on my phone. Instead I should be focused on the potential for relived memories and intertwined hands and healing conversations with a living, breathing human I actually know.

I decide to take a break from social media.

I crave the breezes that used to amble through my brain like the ones that make curtains dance in front of open windows. I miss the mind that wasn't so obedient to people it didn't even know. And I really miss the time before I was constantly low-level irritable because I was jealous, distressed, or buying something.

While philosophers used to meditate on one phrase or word for days or weeks or longer, with social media we consume hundreds of phrases a day, rarely pausing to envision how they fit with the other contents of our brains, and whether they belong at all. They become a part of the permanent collection without so much as a "Hmm."

I don't have a bee in my bonnet over new technology. In fact, one of my favorite history anecdotes is about how Socrates warned that the hot new technology of writing things down would lead to memory loss, inattentiveness, and distraction from wisdom. Ancient writing from Egypt fretted that the new generation and its novel inventions would destroy culture.

Social media is a tool, and you can have a regulated relationship with it. I did not. I mindlessly opened it when I was on a contemplative walk in the forest, and I didn't want to do that anymore.

So I quit all those candy-colored platforms because I realized I am never happy when I go on them. I don't mean that the app doesn't make me happy; I mean that I am never in a good mood when I decide to open it in the first place.

I go to social media when I am agitated, lethargic, absent-minded, lonely, numb, tired, frustrated, bored, or feeling empty in some way. I never go to it because I am in a joyful state of mind. Apps have become an elixir for me to get a quick hit of sensation, yet they rarely offer me any actual sustaining delight or appreciation.

Why was I routinely participating in something that doesn't contribute to my aliveness and, in fact, stopped me from engaging in activities I do enjoy? It isn't fun for me to dislike my own actions. I want to like myself and I want to respect the way I spend my time. Social media was impeding both.

My first few days not being on social media, I felt disoriented, even scared. Mostly because I didn't realize before how much information came to me via those apps before.

The apps are where I learned about pregnancies and job changes, both my friends' and complete strangers'. They're where I learned about what's cool, trendy, and meme-ing. They're where I got a lot of my news stories. They're where I learned the word "unlearning." Without social media, I was missing out on some big personal announcements and breaking news.

But after a short while, I noticed that I was okay with not always knowing what my friends were up to in real time. I was still a part of the group texts, and I much preferred hearing their dispatches directly.

I also liked telling loved ones all my thoughts and feelings about things in person or via phone or email or letters, the way I would back in the old days when I'd write long missives to friends detailing every one of my hopes and hesitancies about a life change.

It was a little weirder to feel out of the loop about news, especially because, in the past few years, I'd noticed a tendency for folks to moralize keeping up with current events, e.g., "You need to check your privilege if you avoid reading the news."

But I quickly came to disagree.

If you measure a person's goodness by their actions to help others, I've definitely become a better person since cutting out news reading from my daily routine.

When I'm not overwhelmed by images and details on every worldwide crisis, doing small things for those around me feels manageable: scooping up an ant in my kitchen and bringing it outside, hauling cans to the food pantry, taking care of senior citizens' pets.

Time-management expert Oliver Burkeman concurs: "You hear it said that it's a marker of privilege to be able to back off from the news—to spend a pandemic planting bulbs in your backyard, or get absorbed in your creative work while democracy declines. But if it really has become a privilege to retain one's sanity, I think it's one the privileged need to exercise, not disavow."

I don't believe we were ever meant to consume so much news. While the benefit is international solidarity, the risk is overwhelming despair. And for me, that possibility of despair completely disrupts my motivation, rather than encourages it.

Maybe the real problem isn't an overabundance of access to information but the invasive nature of information. In both political and spiritual realms, I self-identify as a "seeker." I like going out into the woods or to churches or protests or city alleys and drawing my conclusions from there. I'm a reader, observer, and interviewer—always seeking to understand more about the world we live in.

I don't like the experience of information coming to me. I want to go to it, or at least be surprised by it.

When I find myself maniacally clicking from window to window, repeatedly reacting, a good forest walk will restore my ability to be surprised. Instead of being attacked by digital jolts that seem personally directed at me, I reach toward the birds, trying to connect with them.

When I quit social media, I became an outsider trying to connect. I had to actually ask my friends about their lives; I needed to seek out the news and grapple with my own perspective on it. I had to observe what was cool and trendy rather than be told about it; I had to spend time discerning what my values are instead of being handed them in a bright pink bullet-point list.

During this time, I noticed a difference between "reaction" and "response." I became totally uninterested in reaction—my own, and others'. In the throes of my social media addiction, I looked to the immediate reactions of others to, essentially, tell me how to feel and do the thinking for me. Without that access, I noticed response coming through: the mysterious sacred moments when we are compelled into actions (often unwitnessed by others) or invited into new ways of thinking.

Reaction is cheap. Response is holy.

It's the difference between seeing a painting through a gallery window and pressing my nose up against the glass to visually memorize it versus being force-fed a print sale. It's the difference between underlining a passage in a book that moves me to shiver versus being handed an easily re-grammable graphic of a quote that I'm supposed to find profound. It's the difference between happening upon a street musician who brings me to tears versus the music I never asked for playing in my feed.

Responses are glorious moments, hallowed moments—some of the most significant moments of my life, undocumented (and undocumentable!) on social media.

Here's another small daily distinction between reaction and response.

Almost every day I take the subway, and I never know who I'm going to see on that train. So I pray that God will direct me to the train car I'm supposed to be on for whatever reason and I engage as such. I observe the individuals on the ride with me. I glance around for who might need a seat—even if I mentally grumble while giving mine up. I read the ads, PSAs, and poetry that line the train car, and I wonder what they might have to tell me today.

This is really different from how I used to ride the subway, when I'd scroll and scroll on Instagram to take me myself away from any unpleasantness or humanness that I was experiencing on the train. *Don't let me be reminded of suffering, don't let me feel inferior, don't send me into a spiral of judgment. Take me away, numb me, protect me. I don't want to be here.*

Now I have no other choice but to respond.

In 2001, Barbara Kingsolver wrote about the transition from newspapers to 24/7 TV news, saying that the world has always been this bad; we just know more about it now. In the twenty-plus years since, we now have hundreds of ways to stream graphic, violent, disturbing, even traumatic images straight to our eyes.

And we're not even doing so collectively. Television, at least, was something that communities used to experience together. I remember my mom calling friends on the phone while breaking news slowly unfolded on TV, processing and grieving with a loved one. Now we passively receive shocking images in rapid succession and do so in isolation as we wait for the bus or wake up from sleep.

After doomscrolling for hours, it's so easy to believe the world is a "dumpster fire," as many memes suggest. But when we begin assuming that the world sucks, we're at risk of behaving toward it as such.

At some point, instead of assuming the worst about the goings-on of the galaxy, we have to consciously decide: Do we live in a benevolent universe or not?

Grappling with that eternal question is a holy response, not a cheap reaction.

The first few times the news cycle got really hot while I was off social media, I found myself wanting someone to tell me how to feel about the day's issue. Coming to my own opinion required a lot of thinking (as opposed to looking to my favorite influencers to do the thinking for me!) and the very real possibility of saying the wrong thing.

It was also the first time I felt ownership over my own emotional experience of reading about a conflict a world away. I found that, without the fear of disagreement or internalized pressure to submit to a specific ideology, I could recognize the validity of more perspectives. It wasn't so scary for me to "understand the other side." Rather than instant anger, which performs very well on social media but isn't always sustainable for social progress, I took my time to observe, witness, and ultimately decide what was worth my precious resource of attention. Most often, it was something right in front of me.

Many of my friends didn't understand this perspective. How could I not be consumed with sadness and outrage? How could I neglect to "check in on my [insert demographic here] friend"?

I answered as gently as possible, "I'm not going to obey memes to tell me how to be a friend."

Instead, while the day's conflict was at the top of everyone else's minds, I found myself shifting my gaze to local issues, plus the husband and cat and mom in front of me who needed my engagement and had more invested in me as a person than anything coming from a screen. I wanted to trust in the earth's goodness and beauty again, so I looked out for miracles of nature happening right on the next block.

A year or two ago, I would have been terrified to say such a thing, to step away from my phone. To lift my eyes from the fierce scrutinization of a screen to the small, tender world in front of me.

I had nearly missed the first pink bloom of the magnolia tree around the corner.

In *Being a Human*, Charles A. Foster laments, "We are laughably maladapted to our current lives. . . . We devote to TV brains designed for constant alertness against wolves, and wonder why there's a nagging sense of dissatisfaction."

In a world without the immediate threat of claws and teeth, we find threats in our inbox and on cable news. Screens show real problems, but they do not require the panther-like focus that we willingly donate to them.

Yes, we share the ability to fiercely focus with panthers, and all animals who hunt and are on high alert for danger (which excludes . . . the banana slug?). We've inherited a tremendous skill, the option to block out all noise in order to zero in on something, as my house cat does with a piece of string across the living room.

I wonder how we can use this natural ability for more natural purposes than scrutinizing our former coworker's dinner party, feeling the pain of abandonment after realizing that we weren't invited to a photogenic afternoon picnic, or distressing ourselves with graphic images that block our hearts from hearing a man on the subway asking, "Would anyone like to help me today?"

I'm asking us to train ourselves to pay attention to what's right here, with our body engaged, ready to give our holy response in our own time.

Maybe it begins with a walk in the park, phone in a back pocket. The rustling of the trees and the stirrings of the soul are easier to hear. Those stirrings might be the embryonic flutterings of an idea for a song, or a change, or a revolution.

Save your fierce attention for something that could really use it—those soul stirrings. Like a panther, keep your gaze on the horizon and your ears relaxed and open for the vast majority of the day. Finally, when there's something really juicy in front of you, something rare and special that will feed your heart and mind for days or even years, let your body become an arrow and your eyes become lasers. Then seize, attack, and don't let go.

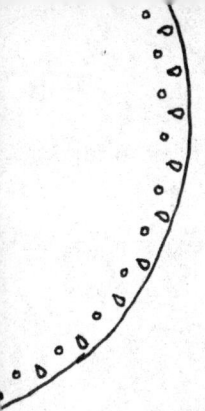

Chapter 4

ON BEARS AND BEING A BODY

There is a morning that I love and celebrate but don't have a name for.

It's the morning when I can feel the earth peel back her blanket and stretch out for the first time in months. For once, she doesn't have to reach for a sweater to throw over her nightgown; she might even step outside to greet the morning.

I do the same, willing my coffee maker to hurry so I can sit on the front stoop and bask in the symphony of new sounds: the silly flap of sandals against the pavement, the no-nonsense buzz of a bee hard at work, the crunch of a bunny snacking on wild flowers. No, that's me getting carried away; there are no bunnies nor wild flowers in my industrial part of Brooklyn.

But there are still new sights to appreciate: people wearing their first sundresses of the season (you all look beautiful!) and the regular café customer switching his order to an *iced* latte and the joggers who smile at one another because it's so much nicer to run in this weather than the surprise storm last week.

Music sounds better. Food tastes sweeter. Problems seem smaller.

I think to myself, *Maybe that wasn't depression. Maybe that was winter.*

It's the first *real* day of spring.

On that first warm day, the one that should be a holiday, I wonder what I was even so sad about for so long; the muddy sludge and slate gray background become a distant memory. The trees seem like they were alive all along. Knobby young buds dot the skeletal branches like babies in cradles. Earth is renewed. My heart quickens its beat.

If you live in bear country and not Brooklyn, the first real day of spring is filled not with joggers and flip-flops but with the grumbles and growls and yawns of drowsy furry beasts emerging from hibernation.

Hibernation isn't sleep. It's a mastery of evolution, a collection of advanced adaptations and seemingly miraculous physiological strategies that allow so many critters to burrow underground for months without food or water and still look like their fuzzy, glorious selves as they totter out of their dens.

Many animals hibernate—marmots, hedgehogs, and bats, to name a few—but bears are the largest and most famous for doing so, perhaps because they look like the type of species that would cozy up for a long winter's snooze. Or maybe I'm just too familiar with the Celestial Seasonings Sleepytime tea illustration of a smiling bear in a gown and sleeping cap dozing off on the family armchair in front of a fire.

After a hearty shake, the animals are rested and ready for action, with healthy, shiny fur coats at that. (When I was in the hospital for a month, in contrast, I emerged looking like a hot mess. I could feel my muscles drooping and bones dwindling; it took a year of intensive exercise to make up for four weeks of inactivity. Not to mention my skin turned a shade of gray I've only seen in instant oatmeal.)

During cold months, bears slow their breathing and heart rate by about 75 percent while maintaining normal body temperature. The boatloads of salmon they demolished during the summer that turned to squishy tummy fat keep them warm as they sleep away the colder months, blood moving dutifully through their veins. And then they resume activity, as though lulled awake by the first blooms of daffodils.

Little kids learn about bear hibernation in school with great fascination. It's a fun fact about a creature world that seems so vastly different from ours. Imagine sleeping for a whole season!

But however wondrous and exotic the ritual seems, hibernation is a challenging concept when you really get to thinking about it: What if humans were just as in tune with our bodies? Would it work out for us? What if we followed our bodily cues as attentively as bears and other animals do?

I finally got around to watching a movie I've read a lot about called *I Saw the TV Glow*. I'm glad I knew going into the film that it's a haunting allegory about transgender identity and the actual horror of having to leave the world you've known in order to transition. (The plot would have confused me otherwise; I'm easily confused.)

As much of a scaredy-cat as I am, I appreciate how the horror genre provides humans with a cathartic exploration of some real-life fears in a contained work of art that we can turn down or turn off when it gets to be too much. But horror movies are overwhelmingly white and heteronormative, and historically haven't reflected the vast range of real-life fears that people of color and queer communities *can't* turn off.

I was curious which real-world fears would make their way into a scary sci-fi nineties-nostalgia-bomb exploring the terror of gender dysphoria, or, as the director described, the egg crack, the moment "when you stop pretending you're not trans, trying to desperately find every reason why you're not, and admit for the first time that you are. That moment can reframe everything in your life."

Of all the shocking, tragic moments throughout the story, the one that really got me was when the main character, Owen, in the throes of dysphoria during late adolescence, is violently vomiting in the bathtub, watched over by his distant and judgmental father.

Owen is retching, sobbing, and screaming: "This isn't my home!!!"

Those words pierced the middle of my belly, a place that I've angrily poked at and pricked countless times with that same sentiment. I don't know what it's like to be trans, but I do know what it's like to feel homesick in my own body because of societal limitations. I know what it's like to scream at my own body and say, "This isn't my home!"

Unlike the character Owen, my bodily disconnectedness didn't come from my own wise intuition within myself; it came from internalizing outside messaging. And when Owen heeded outside messaging, he was not able to be fully at home in his Owenness. That's the case for so many of us (all of us?) who aren't invited to be fully embodied because of some messed-up message or another.

In most of contemporary society, we are practically forced to disembody if we want to have any chance at fitting in, keeping a job, getting accepted, even being seen as fully human.

It is so outrageously not okay yet somehow normal that grocery stores sell "hunger-reducing" gum so that our bodies can't tell us when to eat, and so absurd that we follow a labor schedule that was created for machines, and so upsetting that things like periods and panic attacks and pregnancy are seen as pesky hindrances to be hidden and worked through rather than honored with rest and support.

My first rule at any writing workshop I teach is: *You are a body.*

This means: Make your physical being comfortable, drink when you're thirsty, eat when you're hungry, go to the bathroom when you have to go to the bathroom, squirm, sleep, sulk, slouch . . . whatever your body is nudging you to do.

I say "You are a body" because it took me a long time to learn I am a body. And I want to pass that vital information along to others, especially those who consider themselves creative, i.e., people who "live in their heads" (a strange concept since our bodies contain our heads!).

I, like many others, am a product of a society that splits the mind from the body. Therefore I question my own desires and needs as they arise. I even distrust them, commanding them to keep quiet so I can function normally in this culture that has so many ways to hide bodily requirements.

Something I love about animals is that you never have to tell an animal "Be yourself." They know no other way to be.

A dog has never once had the impulse to withhold an emotion in order to be more palatable, a sparrow has never tried to pass itself off as a parrot, a cat has never held in her hair ball to be ladylike.

Animals go to the bathroom, reject unwanted affection, gobble food, sleep for hours, and bite their toenails without a moment of hesitation or a shameful glance around to see if anyone's looking.

The messages between fuzzy body and little brain don't go through any filtering system. Thought and action are practically one and the same:

Hungry! Eat!

Tired! Rest!

Curious! Explore!

Animals have mastered embodiment, the experience of *being* a body rather than *having* a body. They don't separate their physical self as an unruly object to control, argue with, be proud of, or disdain.

And for a long time, we humans were the same way—not thinking to separate our bodies and minds. That is, until Plato came along and decided that body and mind were two different entities.

Can you blame him? Ancient Greece was a hard place to live. There were wars all the time, rampant slavery, harsh labor, limited resources, and hazards galore when it came to travel.

Plato's coping mechanism to escape the daily grind was by considering the mind the "true self," whereas a body was just a sloppy vessel to carry it around. While bodies were used and hurt by others, and, let's face it, were kind of embarrassing, the mind was pure and could attain enlightenment. Clearly, the feet and the belly button and the other body parts were laughably inferior!

It's an interesting idea, but it's gotten us into all kinds of trouble throughout history. *Dis*embodiment, which denies any inherent preciousness of the body, has been used in service to humanity's most egregious sins, from slavery to eugenics. If you can separate a body from a person, you're more likely to accept the use of that body as an object.

The highly flawed definition of humans as "not animals" is alive and well, and it continues to cause great harm to living things. It justifies the way we thoughtlessly torture and mass eradicate animals in the name of our own agendas, whether we're looking for a compliant test subject to see if nail polish remover damages eyeballs or whether we want cheap milk.

It also means that we endure the legacy of disembodiment as an accepted concept.

Take office jobs, for instance. The nine-to-five workday schedule wasn't made to fit a human body but to fit a human body into the needs of the manufacturing company. A cubicle desk is slightly more comfy than a factory line but often has fluctuating temperatures and limited access to light.

When I worked at an office job—one I actually really enjoyed!—I would get overwhelmed with fatigue every day at about two p.m. I was desperate for a nap in the way thirst made me desperate for water; I daydreamed about sprinting home to sleep.

I thought this meant I was eating the wrong lunch or that I was just weaker than my energetic colleagues who remained bright-eyed and eager even during late-afternoon meetings, when I was basically the person equivalent of scrambled eggs that had been left out too long.

Then I started learning about how men's energy tends to remain at a stable level throughout the day—a significant advantage for the weekday 9–5 schedule. Women's hormones, circadian rhythms, and sleep needs are different. Many of us would probably prefer a schedule of spurts and rests rather than one long block of time.

I imagine most bodies are this way—even men's, seeing as how they are not machines. Getting tired in the middle of the day is a normal human animal activity and not a personality flaw! It's a natural part of being a body that responds to an unknowable amount of environmental and internal fluctuations: brain chemistry, jet lag, a cloudy day, a late night in the pursuit of one more hour spent with favorite people, an early morning due to the anxiety of grief or the birdsong of mourning doves.

I've known people who learned, despite all the conditioning against them, to love and accept *being their bodies*. I wanted that, but it felt like such an abstract concept. I could see other people joyfully living as their bodies, I could mentally work out how it might logically be possible to do, but a wise maxim says: "Knowledge is only a rumor until it is in the muscle."

For a long time, the rumor of embodiment had yet to spread to my muscles. It happened, but it took time.

It took a lot of time learning to love life—not just my life, but the existence of any life on earth. The more I appreciated living things and their living-thing-ness, the more merciful I was toward myself, just as I would be toward a bug who had unknowingly crawled into my kitchen: a living being worthy of mercy for its bug-ness.

Subsequently, I learned to love *signs* of life: eye wrinkles, rolls of fat, chubby cheeks, jiggly arms, laugh lines, stretch marks, cellulite dimples, and colorful veins . . . all signs of vitality, age, changes, growth, and aliveness.

When we hear the word "body," most of us may immediately jump to body image—what our body looks like compared to others'. But what are all the particularities of the body? Why did your soul choose to inhabit your particular physical form?

A viral video that asks fifty adults and children the question "If you could change one thing about your body, what would it be?" reminds us that this is purely conditioning. In the video, adults are asked first. "Only one?" many of them answer with a laugh. Then they answer immediately: smaller ears, bigger ears, shorter forehead, better skin.

The kids, then, have to think a bit harder, and their answers imaginatively enhance their physical abilities—wings to fly, a mermaid tail to swim, a cheetah's running speed, or shark's teeth because they would be cool.

Our childhood selves and our primal creature selves don't scrutinize physical appearance because it doesn't inherently have any currency. It's only when we learn that the way a person looks carries more social power than the way a person feels that we begin longing for bushier eyebrows and a daintier nose.

Asking, answering, reasking, and reanswering the question "Why did my soul choose my body?" has guided me toward my favorite ways of eating, exercising, socializing, and just neutrally existing on a Tuesday afternoon.

I smile when I think about bears who never have to ponder all of this. They eat when they're hungry, wander when they're restless, and sleep when they're tired. Somehow, it all works out. Somehow, after months in a comfy cave, they witness spring as the rest of us do: with energy and renewal. And it's because they never questioned what their bodies needed.

How many ways are we taught to deny our own bodies? Even a cursory list of top-of-mind examples takes my breath away.

I think of my dad, whose teachers beat him when he used his dominant left hand at school.

I think of my friend, a Black man with the personality and demeanor of a newborn kitten, who goes to great lengths to make his body "appear less threatening" in certain spaces (sometimes by carrying a Whole Foods tote, a detail that would be funny if it weren't actually horrifying).

I think about a study on how many five-year-old girls know what dieting is and how to do it.

I think of graduates who change their natural hair texture to look like somebody else's idea of "professional" for a job interview.

I think of people using substances that hinder bodily autonomy.

I think of how many times I got teased for showing emotion.

I think about how many times I went into a toy store and never once wondered if I'd find dolls that looked like me. On any show, in any magazine, I see bodies with hair and skin that resemble mine. I think about what it's like to not have that experience, and it's hard to imagine, but I think about it.

I think of countless ways that our bodies are called "too much" or "not enough," when we're all just ever-changing living things who so deserve to live comfortably at home in our full us-ness.

It helps to get a little guidance. It helps to have a few mirrors. It helps to retrain your brain to recognize beauty in all forms, and it doesn't take long. And for me, it helped to watch a movie that reminded me how far I've come in order to return home—and how badly I wish that everyone could share that journey.

I think about what my soul will miss about being in my body when I die.

I'll miss poking at and squishing my stomach rolls in the bathtub as I have since I was a kid, making funny faces with my belly button as the nose and enjoying the satisfying flop of fat not constrained by clothes as I twist around in search of my loofah.

I'll miss squinting one eye at a time to make the object in front of me move around, a favored bored-in-church activity.

I'll miss running my fingernails gently across the sensitive spread of my inner forearm and then satisfying the tingle with a good scratch.

I'll miss how my bare feet scrunch up a patch of damp grass, how my hamstrings enthusiastically prepare for lift-off when I stand up, how a cold beverage shimmies down my chest, and how my Achilles sighs with pleasure when I press my toes onto the edge of a stairstep and let my calf drop.

I'll miss smelling the clothes of people I love. Hearing a dull pencil scribble on paper (I pray my grandchildren will get to experience the antique contentment of filling out a paper form). Tracing the inside of my ear with a Q-tip. Applying blush. Getting my teeth cleaned (yes). Making myself get even sleepier before a nap so it will feel extra good to doze off. Swimming in a cold lake. Trying to stifle a laugh when it's not appropriate to laugh, which makes me laugh even harder. Riding a bike and pretending it's a horse. Riding a horse and pretending I'm an explorer. Twirling.

The first time I realized all that was the first time I really felt at home here, in me.

I know what it's like to hate this home, and I know what it's like to love being in it.

I know what it's like to feel my body as a brutalist office building made of concrete walls and right angles, restrictions and doors where I didn't know the entrance code.

And I know what it's like to be in my body as a cozy cabin on a lake, next to a forest but not the kind that gets scary at night, and somehow all in the middle of a wild-flower field.

Toward the end of *I Saw the TV Glow*, viewers get a glimpse of what being at home might feel like for Owen. It's a moment of euphoria for character and viewer, but the kind of settled euphoria that you get when you reunite with your best friend or greet your pet upon arrival. Like "OH YEAH, THIS!!!!" The ecstasy of familiarity.

I imagine that's how my cat feels when she stretches her long body and flexes her paws, a thrilling reminder that she is a cat. When I splash around a pool, more attentive to my soul's elation than to the shape of my being in a bathing suit, I am thrillingly reminded that I am a Mari.

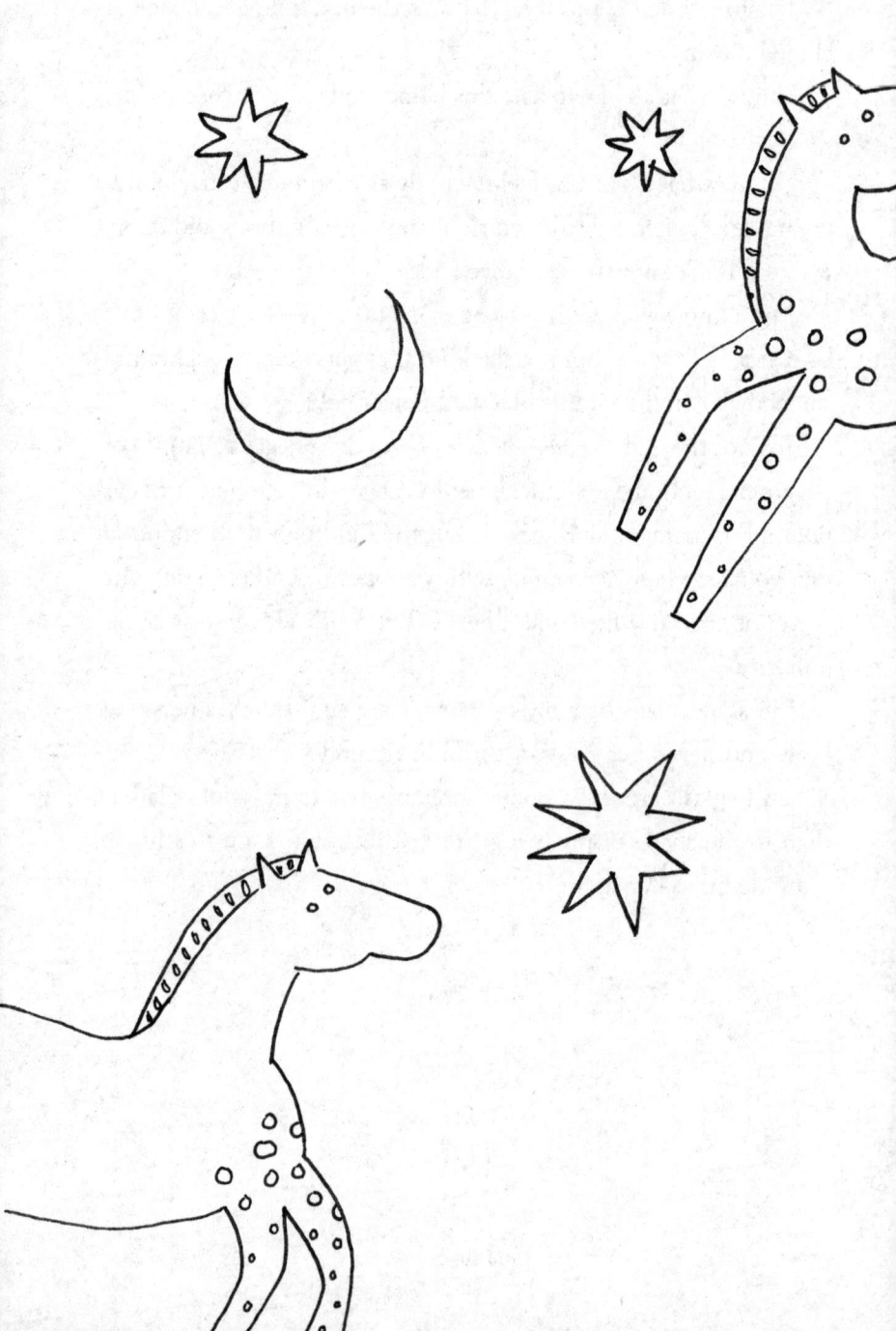

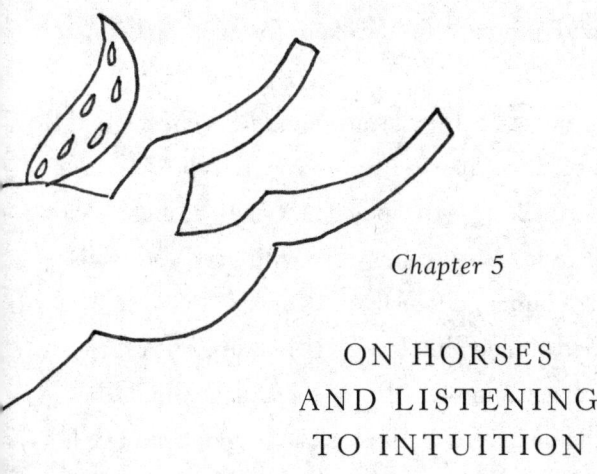

Chapter 5

ON HORSES
AND LISTENING
TO INTUITION

When I first started my hospital chaplain internship, I thought I was going to nail it.

I knew grief, I knew sickness, I knew hospitals, I knew about spiritual crises. I boldly came in envisioning that I was going to have the right words for every possible scenario, like a human version of a book of Thích Nhất Hạnh quotes.

My first day, I entered the room of a guy around my age, curled in a cashew shape on top of a bed covered with stains. At the sight of someone in actual pain—not one of the illustrated examples from the chaplain handbook—I wanted to leave immediately. Instead, I gulped through my discomfort and introduced myself as my mentor instructed me to do: "Hi, I'm Mari, I'm the chaplain on this floor, how's it going today?"

He looked up at me and moaned. "Not good."

I took a breath and announced, "I'm here for emotional support."

Theo (so said the name on the placard hanging from his bed frame) stared at me blankly, then started to cry. Except it wasn't the type of cry I was expecting—the movie kind with a single tear and restrained sniffles. It was a leaden sob, with snot and wails and the whole menu of human anguish.

His reaction startled me and I became extremely uncomfortable, which is sort of the exact opposite of how a chaplain should be. Not only did I feel shame in seeing him look so despondent, but I immediately felt bad about not being able to help in the moment. I desperately wanted to alleviate his agony.

Maybe I said a quick prayer? I don't remember the rest because I was so nervous and awkward and suspected that I'd probably made his day even worse by the time I left.

In other words, I did not nail it.

My mentor Ruth, a no-nonsense, grey-haired, Birkenstocks-wearing rabbi with tons of political pins on her backpack who was easily irritated by hubris, told me, "You *don't* know. Even if you had the patient's exact illness, or you've felt the same way, you don't know what it's like to be them. Enter their room only with questions, never answers." (On my first day, she also scolded me for wearing sensible-ish kitten heels: "You're not going to be able to get around the hospital in those shoes!")

Over the next six months of my internship, I visited hundreds of rooms in the ICU, beginning each interaction with, "Hi, I'm Mari, I'm the chaplain on this floor, how's it going today?" And then I'd sit in a room full of beeping machines, listening to whatever the patient felt like sharing with a stranger that day.

It was so hard for me not to offer up anything. I've been through enough that I know I shouldn't try to find a bright side, explain away the pain, or say "I know how you feel," but it was extremely uncomfortable to sit with someone my age who was dying, or with the family member of someone who'd just got ten very bad news. I was in the position of helping them, and I thought that help meant I had to offer something. I had to leave them with a nugget, a mantra, something brilliant to soothe and uplift them.

But then I got to thinking about it: When you're in the hospital, everyone who comes into your room is sure about one thing or another. Doctors tell you what you have, nurses tell you what to do, family and friends tell you how to feel.

I get why.

It feels so, so good to be a sage, so good in fact that I can easily see the appeal of being a cult leader. For someone like me, I get a hit of euphoric superiority when I'm able to give advice or share a story that makes sense of everything: I make meaning for a living and I fancy myself spiritually in tune. Since I was a kid, many older people have told me "It's not your first time on earth." I'm proud of this.

But chaplaincy humbled the hell out of me because the hospital is a place where nothing makes sense. There's no wisdom in a hospital room; there's just lonely beeping and chaos. Good people can pray really hard and never see a miracle; others get out easy for no apparent reason at all.

During one of our training sessions, Rabbi Ruth showed us a stunning documentary called *Buck* about a "horse-whispering" cowboy who learned to communicate with traumatized, aggressive, or "untrainable" horses through learning their personalities and histories. Before his novel approach, the norm was to beat the animals into submission with little interest in discovering what made them act the way they did. Ruth played the movie to drive home the importance of individualizing our approach to chaplaincy rather than using a one-size-fits-all method.

Horses are an unusual domestic animal because they remain highly attuned to their environment, even when they live in controlled conditions. Because horses were bred as prey animals, their survival historically depended on their ability to perceive subtle environmental and emotional cues and react accordingly. Horses respond to the slightest squeeze of your leg, hear the softest whisper of trees, and sense the smallest fly land on their shoulders.

The same remarkable sensitivity that makes them extra wary of danger makes them extra tricky to train. It takes a lot of time and care to desensitize them to certain sensations. Rookie riders might flap objects within eyeshot of their horses to prepare them for such terrors as a rustle in the bushes or a plastic bag tumbling across the road, only to find that their horse loses trust in this unreliable weirdo who will startle him with flapping objects.

Even a horse who's been ridden a million times won't respond well to a human who's ultranervous and angry, erratic and irritable. In fact, horses emulate human emotions, acting as a mirror for our behavior.

This is why they can be such good therapists for those suffering from post-traumatic stress disorder (PTSD) and other mental-health afflictions: horses require consistency, calm, and trust in order to behave consistently, calmly, and trustingly. Those who have mental afflictions must develop more awareness and skills to manage their emotions in order to bond with their horse. The animal beautifully reflects its client's progress; as the person becomes more confident, so does the horse.

Horse therapy isn't a new tradition by any means. Hippocrates wrote about the healing power of horses in ancient Greece, touting "riding's healing rhythm." Early medical practitioners would prescribe horseback riding to those with incurable diseases. I wonder if those "incurable diseases" included psychological torments that doctors puzzled over. I wonder how many lives have been saved by the nuzzle of an animal who witnessed a person's cries, numbness, distrust, and despair.

Over time, with patient after patient, I began to realize that the role of the chaplain is to hold hands in the dark, not to search around with a flashlight in order to find the light switch. An offer to share the darkness can be a valuable gift when everyone else is forcing fluorescence on you.

I learned to mirror the patients' feelings, using language tricks so simple it felt like cheating.

Patient: "I'm really scared."

Me: "This seems really scary."

And so forth.

I think it must be refreshing to hear "I don't know what it's like to be you, and I don't know what's going to happen." I imagine it can be a relief to hear the truth, which is that nobody really knows.

I'd like to think that having even such simplistic interactions may feel radical to someone who up until then has only been told "Don't be scared."

On one of my last days, I sat with a woman who was going through a lot of emotional pain on top of the physical pain: marriage troubles and financial woes, plus a really frustrating medical condition. "I'm a good person," she assured me, and recited an autobiography confirming her thesis. "I've had a hard life and I've always been good. So why this?"

Trust me, I wanted so badly to teleport out of there as soon as I could. But instead I just sighed along with her. A co-sigh. "It's unfair," I said. "It makes no sense." When I said that, I could tell that she trusted me a little more. She softened and was able to laugh.

I imagine what makes someone an effective chaplain is similar to what makes horses great for people suffering from PTSD or mental illness. Someone feels worried and can palpably feel the horse affirming, *You feel worried.*

The horse mimics fear, hypervigilance, even numbness. In a

world that is demanding a PTSD sufferer "get back to normal," the horse simply reflects what is already there. In a world that tells depressed people to "snap out of it," the horse simply affirms what is already there. How healing it can be to hear the truth.

"You're going through so much," I learned to say to the patients, admittedly as a method to help them open up.

"Yeah," they all answered in one way or another. "I really am."

I imagine that so many people suffering with their mental health have felt that same understanding around their assigned horse. "Yeah," in response to whatever emotion the horse was demonstrating. "I really am."

At the hospital, I learned that Western society is pathetic when it comes to the act of suffering.

We have such limited vocabulary for the many types of losses we experience throughout life and such a limited imagination when it comes to our support systems.

Only a handful of people "get" to fully grieve the loss of someone close to them, but how many others are acutely sharing that grief? I'm thinking about how beloved friends of the deceased don't necessarily get to take their three allotted bereavement days from work because they're not family members. I'm thinking about the pals who don't receive updates from the doctor on a buddy's medical condition because the friends haven't passed some sort of closeness test.

In my time as a chaplain, I became so aware of how much we suck at providing space for grief and suffering that doesn't fit into one small, square gift box with a bow.

How about the man I visited in the emergency maternity wing as his wife screamed with pain during her miscarriage? He took me aside and wondered how on earth he was going to get through this, since he couldn't find any support groups for men who feel the pain of miscarriage too. What direction could I have given him?

Or what about the woman who was closer to her dance troupe than her family and wanted them to come give a performance for her as she slipped out of life? Where could I place her longing, when only relatives were invited to visit her deathbed?

Or what do I do with myself when, after over four years, one of my best friends is still minimally conscious after emergency brain surgery? What do I do with all my love for her, how do I process my grief, what words and what feelings do I assign to this ambiguous loss that, according to the hospital's offering of resources only for family members, isn't even fully mine to process?

Pain scares other people, even if they've been through it before—like me! It's confronting and distressing to look at someone who is going through real agony for which there is no easy fix. How helpless us humans feel when a friend tells us they're enduring a hard time with no hope in sight, or when our family member's body begins failing. How desperate we are to say, "You'll be okay!" As though our loved one can be kept from the truth.

That's why the presence of someone who isn't there to fix anything is so necessary and comforting. For many of us, that's an animal.

A horse might be the only being in the life of a person with PTSD or mental illness who isn't actively trying to fix them, wish it away, pray it better, or deny that it exists.

The animal keeps telling the truth.

You're irritable. You're distrustful. You're distracted. You're hurting me. A horse will never hide from you what you are feeling. And it won't walk away from your cry but will stay there until you're finished and ready to ride.

When I was considering the path of chaplaincy, I talked with a priest friend of mine who used to serve as chaplain in an infant ICU.

She told a story of a father who visited his ill infant daughter every day, many hours a day, during which he would simply look at her. There's no telling what was going through his head as he watched her: Awe? Adoration? Despair?

He watched her grow and die at the same time, as long as he could.

My friend shed tears as she pondered that maybe this is how God watches us, unable to take away our pain but wholly in touch with it. The father couldn't deny or change what horror was unfolding in front of him; he could merely be a witness to it.

This is how I've come to think about companionship in general.

I am a witness to my friends' lives, and they are a witness to mine. And what higher calling is there for two partners than to bear witness to each other's comings and goings and foibles and triumphs?

When I spent a month in the hospital as a patient with an autoimmune disease that almost entirely paralyzed me from the neck down, it seemed so backward that I would be evaluated only by my physical changes and not on the growth of my soul during that time.

And when I told nurses that I was a writer and artist with a vibrant social life, it felt like I was talking about the alternative universe of my own life, one in which I was still able to use my hands to draw and my feet to dance.

How I ached to have witnesses to both states.

It feels necessary to be witnessed, as though the desire for a bystander is baked into human DNA. We want to be seen, heard, felt, smelled, tasted, and touched, and we find all sorts of ways to do that: to force our homemade lasagna upon dinner guests, to extend our hands in welcome, to douse ourselves in perfume, all with the hope of being thought about later by others.

Whenever I visited a patient and their prognosis was so bleak that I had absolutely nothing to say, I would simply witness and provide evidence of it.

"You have beautiful green eyes."

"This is really frustrating for you."

"Is this a picture of Anna?"

"What do you miss most about Seoul?"

"I know you can't talk, and I can't imagine how hard that must be, but I'm asking your family all about you and I'm learning who you are."

The etymology of "companion" is "someone to eat bread with." It's as basic an act as watching over, waiting for, and listening to. It makes me wonder if "companionship" could be a verb for "to witness each other." I believe cowitnessing is what wedding vows are about, and it's also what the community aspect of end-of-life rituals is about.

Watch, wait, listen, witness, repeat.

This is the "use" that animals so frequently serve for people. On a particularly chaotic day in the hospital, I helped usher a therapy rabbit, Cinnamon, around to different rooms on the neurology floor for anyone who had lost some of their ability to communicate with loved ones. Cinnamon just sat there and existed while patients spoke to her in half-finished phrases. I've cried myself to sleep as my cat sits at the opposite end of the bed, understanding only the universal language of grief. But unlike a person, she doesn't tell me I'll get over it. She just witnesses it, which is all I need.

While humans—including me as a rookie chaplain—so often fumble through clunky words searching for a way to say, "I am here," animals effortlessly embody the phrase. It would take a lifetime to learn how to be as good a chaplain as a horse who simply witnesses.

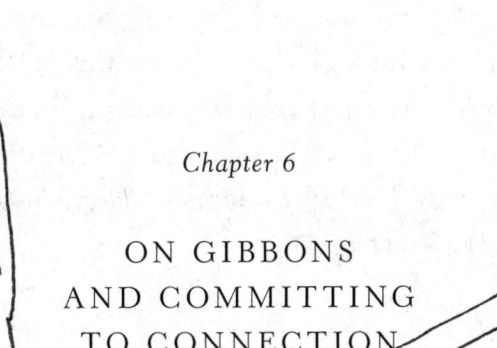

Chapter 6

ON GIBBONS
AND COMMITTING
TO CONNECTION

On a misty evening in October, when fog played hide-and-seek for hours around the Manhattan Bridge, I got married at a local restaurant right on the water. I loved every second of wedding planning—getting to choose burgundy ranunculus for the table, George Michael for the dance playlist, some grapefruit tequila potion for the signature cocktail, a Walt Whitman poem for the ceremony reading, Spanish lace for my veil, and gold glitter polish for my manicure. My inner child had a field day.

The only sticky part was when I asked my fiancé about my walking-down-the-aisle song. I gave him full rein when it came to most of the music, but this one seemed more personal, like it should land in the sliver of our Venn diagram of taste, which was already fairly slim.

After a stroke of emotion during a tough, punk-fueled workout, my fiancé suggested the Blink-182 hit "All the Small Things," a rock love song about appreciating the little gestures that keep a relationship strong. Growing up, I could never avoid Blink-182—their influence was everywhere, and I was under their spell for a few formative years. The song choice was so sweet and sentimental, I immediately passed it along to our musicians, who would create a gorgeous rendition of it.

The song choice compromise reminded me of a fact I once learned about gibbons, little agile apes who live in many countries of Asia. They are one of the few mammals who mate for life, but even sweeter than that, they share a special song. Over time, mated gibbons will combine their individual mating calls into a "duet," finding harmony between their vocal cries and creating a signature song, the cornerstone of their partnership. Like many lovers, they'll serenade each other during intimate moments of grooming, and they'll call each other back home through that familiar ballad. It reminds me of pre-internet teenagers phoning in to a radio show to request a pop hit in dedication to their special someone.

I was so tickled to learn that a creature who can mate for life (like humans) also shares a song for life. It confirmed to me what came intuitively, that couples (or friends, or families!) create their own culture built from language, gestures, codes, preferences, styles, and traditions. I was excited to cherish this Blink-182 song as much as the gibbons cherished their own mating song.

I wasn't surprised when a lot of people assumed that wedding planning was stressful and hard and overwhelming.

"It's so fun, such a treat!" I countered.

Our friends praised us for being so chill, and our ideas for being so simple, and our walking-down-the-aisle song for being so perfectly, impossibly "the two of us."

I did not, however, expect so many people to ask *why* I was getting married in the first place.

Could "It's so fun, such a treat!" work for this legal and religious commitment that now seems clunky and outdated, oppressive and patriarchal? No. During my short engagement, I realized I needed a more compelling motive to appease my skeptical friend group.

Months after the wedding, I found myself in the middle of Wyoming. Literally, if you looked on a map of the US, I was smack-dab in the middle of the square-shaped state. I was about to teach writing for a week and had no idea where exactly I was or what exactly I was doing. "One breath at a time," I told myself, especially as my breaths felt bigger out on those sprawling rangelands.

In my memory, specific images stick out: a razor-blue clear sky stretching between red canyons that looked like popsicles melting into grass, a horse with two different-colored eyes, a campfire swallowing twigs whole, and town names on signs with punch-line population numbers . . .

BASIN, WYOMING: POPULATION 1,311

MANDERSON, WYOMING: POPULATION 88

OTTO, WYOMING: POPULATION 50

As the cab from Cody (population 10,224) drove me to Hyattville (population 46), I collected these town names in memory so I could look them up later, but their digital footprints led to little more than census facts.

I wanted to know what it's like to go to school for twelve years with the same dozen kids, and how the broad landscape expands one's internal world, and where the grocery store is, and whether people choose to stay.

Alas, I'd just have to do what we did before the internet: wonder.

I'd been wondering a lot about small towns lately as my interest in interideological dialogue (i.e., talking to people with different viewpoints) had been increasing day by day.

And I'd been wondering if maybe small towns possess the key to the opposite of loneliness.

Presumably (with full acknowledgment of how easy it is for me to romanticize), lifetime dwellers in a small town need to figure out their conflicts over the years. In a town of forty-six, there aren't too many places to avoid your neighbors.

Heck, even in a town of 10,224.

Before heading out to Hyattville, I stayed a night in Cody, which has its own airport and farm-to-table Lebanese food.

It also has a tight-knit community of people who love the outdoors, and that spans from proud NRA members to vegans with wildcrafted tincture stands: hunters meet hippies.

Both share appreciation for the land, skepticism of government, comfort in the forest, and apparent enthusiasm for window decals. You'd think they could work something out together. And they probably do.

People of vastly different political and social leanings *have* to hang out together (or at least side by side) in Cody, unless I'm grossly underestimating a person's ability to frequent only one restaurant for their entire life.

Those in big cities can be a lot more selective about who they interact with on a given day. And I'm curious if that's contributing to the international epidemic of loneliness.

Before I left for Wyoming, I had a fascinating conversation with Amanda, a playfully wise friend and our wedding officiant. Amanda's been working in peace education at Vassar College after years of studying social change and reconciliation. She pondered:

"One thing I was wondering about today is how the world is exponentially increasing in people, and we also have these devices now that give us infinite access to infinite amounts of individuals, and we also are more mobile than we've ever been in history, and the globalization of the economy means that our jobs move around. . . . Yet we are in a loneliness epidemic. It's so interesting as a person who studies relationships, bonds, forgiveness, reconciliation . . . that we struggle so much.

"And I sometimes wonder if it's because of the illusion of infinite options—always other fish in the sea—and this idea of 'I could always go somewhere else. I could always meet other people. I can just stop talking to someone I'm upset with and find a new friend group.'"

She told me that her students on campus can sometimes get so upset when there's interpersonal conflict that they would rather cut a peer off than engage with them and try to work out some sort of resolution.

Sounds like someone I know. (Me!!)

This is when we both started wondering about itty-bitty towns.

Back when we had smaller communities and tended to stay in one place, getting along with people we didn't agree with must have been necessary for us to survive. In the face of a common enemy or in war, you would have had to get along with someone even if you didn't like the person, or even if they made you feel bad about yourself!

In the past, we must have had to learn how to continue to live with one another. Or who knows, there's the Romeo and Juliet option where we just all die?!

Amanda and I are both avid world travelers, and we're both grateful that we're not forced to stay in one place. We have also both experienced relationships that we absolutely needed to leave.

And yet our conversation about staying with people was rich and layered.

We agreed it's a good thing that people are more mobile in relationships when they're abusive, but we also don't want to destroy or excommunicate (i.e., cancel) anyone because they've been abusive—which usually means they've been abused themselves.

And we both have a special love for our friendships that have withstood ups and downs, highs and lows. Those are the strongest relationships because they have weathered disagreements.

We started wondering how much of our global loneliness is directly linked to a growth in hypermobility. If there's no reason or need to commit, then why do it? Why not just seek other people who see things the same way we do, articulate them using the same words, or feel them with the same level of passion?

Well, maybe because commitment is the opposite of loneliness.

To commit to someone in marriage, we realized, was a radical act in 2024! And, yes, potentially stifling, and heteronormative, but also how radical to commit to another person fully. Or a place! How many of us have the capacity to do that these days? How many of us can say that we're going to be in a place for a long period of time, and that our job or another need isn't going to move us?

The whole conversation made me fall in love all over again with this radical concept of commitment—something I took very seriously during the depths of the pandemic, when I stayed in New York.

I've always been a commitment-phobe.

My friends used to joke that as soon as I moved to one city, I'd begin packing for the next. I change my mind a lot. I like to follow my whims. I value flexibility and spontaneity. I won't even sign up for a ceramics class if it's longer than eight weeks.

But when I moved to New York seven years ago, I knew I couldn't mess this relationship up. I wanted to spend the rest of my life with this city, so, like with any relationship, I'd have to give it plenty of attention and signs that I was in it for the long haul.

After a year of spending my Sunday mornings at brunch or making up for lost sleep, I decided I wanted to go to a church. I'd show New York that I was here to stay by finding a weekly anchor.

I expected to do a bit of church shopping, but I knew right away that Trinity Lower East Side had some serious potential: it had the Progress Pride flag waving outside, the word "inclusive" all over the website, an obvious devotion to feeding the hungry, and, just as alluring, it was a couple of blocks from my apartment.

All of a sudden, I've been going every Sunday for years. Friends have moved in and moved out, I've changed neighborhoods and peer groups, I've cried over loss and I've celebrated my engagement, and, all the while, I've seen and talked to the same community every week.

By no means is my church full of all my best friends in one room; it's an intergenerational and intercultural stew of leftovers from all us side dishes that got kicked out of the main course. Weirdos and misfits galore, your girl right at home among them. But I know when something inevitably nightmarish happens to me, they will be there for me, and I for them.

I joyfully greet people every week whom I know next to nothing about, who on paper have next to nothing in common with me. And yet I'm 100 percent committed to them.

Is commitment the opposite of loneliness?

I was talking to my seventy-four-year-old mom about loneliness the other week. While so many people her age feel it starkly, she doesn't. Even though she is a recent widow who moved cities just a couple of years ago, she doesn't get lonely.

And I have a theory as to why: She has commitments. She has weekly phone calls, regular check-ins, active group texts, and daily recap emails from yours truly.

It's not just about having friends; I've experienced many years of loneliness even with a good amount of friends. It's about committing to people and having them commit to you, which is just rare these days, no two ways about it. Perhaps it's because our culture greatly values an individual's feelings before commitment.

In a lot of ways, this is a good thing. In some ways, maybe it's missing something. After all, tons of arranged marriages are really successful on every level, including joy. And I've gained so much from the traditions of yoga and church, where you go whether you're feeling or believing it or not.

Often, when we reflect on belonging, we remember how it felt when we belonged, or we think about times we felt silenced, unheard, didn't belong. We think about how terrible or wonderful those feelings felt. And sometimes, we believe that the way to get back to the place of security, inclusion, belonging, or being heard is to be in the safest possible space. Often for us that means we're with people who think and act and respond to stimuli similarly ("affinity spaces," so called in diversity work).

What's paradoxical about that impulse is that, in order for peace, justice, survival to work, we need to manage relationships across difference. We have to work *with* people. Which doesn't just mean tolerating them—it means figuring out forms of collaboration in order to, as scholar Donna Haraway says, "render each other capable," say, of surviving a climate crisis or reaching a ceasefire agreement.

What's funny about the belief that we can only reach consensus when everyone has the same position is that we don't realize how our differences render us more capable. What we're failing to realize is that it's our differences that make a lot of the work we do possible. The trite idea of diversity is our strength.

Now, don't get it twisted. . . . Do I love these ideas in theory? Absolutely. Do I love these ideas in practice? Hello, I am a human and I absolutely do not! Even as someone who is super interested in this work, I find myself *swiftly* mentally canceling acquaintances as soon as I feel a threat: the incorrect bumper sticker, a suspicious social media follow, evidence of a stop at a fast-food chain whose CEO has questionable ideology.

But I recognize that not only does that set me up for close-mindedness, it also sets me up for loneliness. This radical idea of commitment helps unlonely myself, but I can't only commit to people I agree with all the time, or I will only be committed to my nonverbal houseplants. And they are mostly dead.

I don't know for sure if the folks in small-town Wyoming have avoided loneliness, but they have achieved something that strikes me as unusual in this age: commitment to place and people, even on the hard days.

It's so cute that gibbons create a song with their mate-for-life, but it's also something quite profound, and radical: no matter what the mate is feeling that day, how he's behaving, what he's standing for, there will be one single song that draws him back to his mate, community, and home.

When I feel the most distant from my neighbor or even my own kin, what is the song that will bring us back together?

Chapter 7

ON ZEBRAS
AND STAYING SAFE
IN COMMUNITY

Like most July mornings, I started this one at Tompkins Square Park. A sudden storm that woke me up in a full-body jolt at three-ish a.m. had washed the East Village clean, so the air was already fat and rich at sunrise, smelling of farmers' market herbs.

I opened the wrought iron gate of the park, scaring a squirrel as the hinge squeaked. I took off my shoes and carried them along with my book and a blanket to the middle of the grass and began assembling my reading area.

That's when the park's residents began getting up.

Not the animal residents—they'd been busy all morning pecking at worms who had emerged from the wet soil after the storm.

The human residents began unzipping their tents, one by one. They slowly crawled out like bears after hibernation, squinting and stretching, extending one limb out before fully standing up, zipping the tents behind them.

If the park were a cathedral, they would be the statues of saints with dazed expressions lining the aisle toward the altar that was the spectacular elm tree at the end of the lawn.

There was nothing else saintly about this group, except perhaps for the way they looked after one another.

"I'm going to go take a shit at Starbucks, watch my stuff," one of the older men growled to the group. A couple of them drowsily nodded.

Crassness aside, his ask was less of a command and more of an invitation, probably something he invited them to do for him dozens of times a day: Take care of him. Watch over him. And they did.

This is one of several tent communities in the East Village. This particular one has existed in various forms, and been cleared countless times, since the 1980s when parents forbade their children from walking across the park lawn and political activists mingled with marijuana dealers and punk rocker activists clashed with police to protect the encampments.

These days, the people living in those tents constantly live in fear of yet another surprise "sweep," a euphemism for a forced removal of their tents and belongings, plus pets if they have them.

City officials will justify the sweeps in the name of safety, even dignity: "This is no way for people to live, and they should be moved off the streets and into shelters with the goal of permanent housing."

Others, including everyone in the Tompkins Square Park encampment, call the tents their homes and don't want to move. "If we'd rather live in a tent than in a shelter, imagine how bad the shelters are," one of them tells a passerby midsweep. They prefer the term "unhoused" to "homeless," because, simply, they have a home—it's just a tent.

Many believe that the city's real agenda is to keep tents from interfering with tourism. There's good reason to suspect as much: During the Atlanta, Georgia, preparations for hosting the 1996 Olympics, the mayor did a sweep while passing stricter panhandling and loitering ordinances. The Atlanta police arrested countless unhoused people weeks before the first Olympian arrived.

Sweeps increase in parts of Florida just before peak tourist season. In Los Angeles, individuals who have created a neighbor network of functioning homes are suddenly the targets of police for "loitering" and find themselves spending a weekend in a cell, wondering what happened to their friends and their dog.

As I spread myself out on the blanket, tummy down, feet up, I watched a couple make "camp coffee" outside their tent, straining the grounds from a can of Café Bustelo through a damp paper towel into a tin pot. Another person ripped open a plastic bag of small apples and handed them out, chomping one in half as he dangled the bag in front of his neighbors. One by one they left to use a coffee shop bathroom or pick up anything that had been left in the community fridge outside the food pantry; today there was a jar of maraschino cherries, a frozen bag of mixed vegetables, and a black trash bag full of loose carrots—presumably left from a nearby restaurant.

Soon, the humidity began setting in and the air became stuffed and salty.

One of the men left for work at nine, wiping his brow with his sleeve. His job was in New Jersey so his friends looked after his tent all day, in shifts. Another returned from work; he was the night janitor at a mall and his uniform had certainly seen better days.

One woman with a white globe of puffy dandelion hair began setting up a sidewalk art sale, taping a sign to the park fence that listed her paintings of neon aliens and geometric swirls on squares of cardboard for ten dollars each.

The tent dogs idly played, and the one cat on a small pink leash stretched before going back to sleep in the sun.

Other folks from beyond the park joined me on the lawn over the course of the hot morning: a man in a crisp white shirt unfolded a beach chair and opened his laptop; some teenage girls used their sweatshirts as blankets to lie down on and gossiped over iced coffee and cigarettes.

And, for now, the tents stayed put, a row of colorful domes with the backdrop of a gentrifying neighborhood in a city that wished they would just go away.

Most herd animals watch out for one another, and even watch out for other species. Conservationists have observed elephants protecting injured or orphaned rhinos from predators, such as lions, and keeping them company. Vampire bats, bloodthirsty creatures of the night that they are, will feed other bats at a cost to their own well-being; they (generously and disgustingly) regurgitate their dinner for a bat who didn't get any food that day. When a goose gets hurt during migration, at least one goose will stay close by until it heals or dies. Across the wildlife kingdom, it seems like we're hardwired to share and give what we can.

Of course, territorial instinct often competes with an inclination toward compassion. Chimps may adopt orphans within their own group but you'll rarely see a chimp colony offer grace to a neighboring community; it's all-out war if a young primate so much as wanders into the wrong part of the jungle.

This tension transfers neatly into the human kingdom, particularly in modern cities where supposed supporters of affordable housing cry "Not in my backyard!" when they discover the proposal for a new public housing complex that will be down the street from them. Well-meaning parents may take their kids out of an underperforming public school at the expense of the rest of the school's children. We all have limitations to our compassion, but true community demands that we fully live out our interconnectedness and believe that we all belong to one another.

For inspiration, we have no further to look than to zebras.

Zebras demonstrate a standard of coliving that would make Wendell Berry—the poet champion of local interdependent communities—jump up in standing ovation. While pop psychology may call them "codependent" (they can't and won't sleep unless they're accompanied by members of their pack!), their cooperation with one another for the sake of harmonious side-by-side living is marvelous to behold.

Maybe it's because they're in a lot of danger all the time. Zebras aren't exactly kill machines like big cats or thunderous hippos. They're essentially goofy-looking horses with Mohawks and long tongues that hang out like Gene Simmons's. Easy prey. And they don't have spikes or razor teeth or tusks or horns, so their only real defense is one another.

Zebras live and migrate in large groups, taking on new members without much fuss. A group of zebra wives has been known to treat any new girl with skepticism and even hostility, but like all knitting circles and dance troupes before them, they eventually bond with the newbies.

And once you're in, you're *in*. Zebras defend one another fiercely, forming a giant circle around any member of their herd who's being attacked by a predator. *Not on my watch*, you can imagine them saying.

Zebras develop reliable shifts to protect one another while they eat and sleep, taking turns to make sure someone's on the lookout at all times. I imagine them like kids who stand outside the bathroom for one another, or who distract a parent while the others grab more snacks from the pantry.

As they migrate in search of more food, which is pretty much constantly, zebras are keenly aware when a herd member goes missing. They will hold up their traveling schedule in order to call out and hunt for the lost creature—even the ones they don't know very well. If one is lost or in danger, they don't rely on the remaining strength in numbers to get them across the Serengeti in one piece. They know that if one goes, it affects the entire herd.

Their reliance on one another is probably long established in their DNA. Zebras weren't designed to be alone, quite literally.

Their stripes do no good by themselves and would be a liability if one zebra were to take a solo walkabout away from the group. The black-and-white patterns that look like a baffling display to a predator when a zebra is in a herd quickly change to the equivalent of a sign that reads HEY, LOOK AT ME! when a zebra is alone.

Zebras also cooperate with the local ostrich community on the plains. Ostriches and zebras are both popular prey for faster animals and they trade information to stay alert to predators. Ostriches have glorious eyesight and a built-in lookout tower that is their long necks, whereas zebras have enviable hearing in ears that can rotate in multiple directions. The two travel close together in an unexpected buddy pairing, the communities braiding together during migration.

To be a zebra is to need and be needed by others. You'll never see a zebra going rogue, embarking on a quixotic quest toward independence. No, their driving purpose is to protect and be protected, feed and be fed, groom and be groomed, watch out and be watched out for.

"I'm afraid I'm getting codependent," I admitted to my therapist.

Nearly laughing, she replied, "How can you not be right now?"

In the aftermath of the pandemic, it turns out we humans needed one another more than ever. Or maybe we've always needed one another the same amount, but this time we weren't able to pretend otherwise. There are moments in an individual's life and in a society's history when the jig is up: we can't do this alone.

I used to have a series of puzzles where the pieces fit together to show an ideal scene in color of a ballet performance, a magnificent castle, an art museum. As you removed the pieces, the background board had a black-and-white sketch to show the same image, but this time it was behind-the-scenes. So, the prima ballerina would be practicing in her leotard while a scene painter stood on a tall ladder to the side and her choreographer scolded her move. The castle puzzle showed all the workers who hustle to create a serene home for its habitants. The art museum revealed a night crew who clean and adjust before the next day's batch of visitors comes in.

The years following the pandemic reminded me of one of these puzzle removals, except this one showed the ailing spiritual, mental, and social health of our city and far beyond. Many people who appeared to be "doing fine" were propped up by professional help or slumped onto the crutch of medication. People endured chronic loneliness and tremendous grief. There were underpaid workers, struggling families, people who until then had never had to line up at a food pantry.

Maybe the puzzle still had a couple of pieces of the color facade showing, but the background was also on display, our frailties and scaffolding coming into the foreground.

At the same time, I also became aware of social media and self-help books that advocate for individual healing before entering into a relationship or even a friend group. "Work on yourself," I heard over and over as advice for how to get a boyfriend, how to make friends, how to get an invite to a book club, how to be a healthy member of society and not leak your toxic-trait goo all over the people you meet.

"Red flags" in dating memes often include lines like "If he hasn't been to therapy . . ." or "If he hasn't healed his childhood wounds . . ." as though any potential partner must arrive formed, whole, and perfect, like an enlightened doll off the assembly line with a shiny smile in the face of any setback.

But people don't work this way. You could be in therapy for twenty years and still be susceptible to countless triggers and insecurities (ask me how I know this). Sometimes the real healing actually begins in relationships with others, when you learn how to trust-fall into caring arms that will hold both your beauty and brokenness.

It's not only in regard to romantic relationships that I've seen the demand for an impossible standard of wholeness, but also in communities and friendship circles. While it's easy to see our culture of disposability play out when conferences are stocked with plastic water bottles and throwaway champagne glasses, it takes more time to realize that we've begun to treat people in our lives as disposable too.

We can justify dropping a "toxic" friend in the name of good boundaries or leaving a group without a trace because we have "higher standards." In the dating world, swiping right and left on faces with full life histories behind them trains us well for this. If you don't like something about this person, you can use your finger to toss them aside and you never have to look at them again!

But just like those plastic champagne glasses, humans go somewhere. If they're out of your sight and mind, they're in someone else's sight and mind. And then what is our responsibility?

When the city sweeps another encampment, perhaps it is

"disposing" of people in that neighborhood, but those people don't disappear. What's left is a haunted neighborhood with a gaping hole where a resilient and caring community once lived—now dispersed all over zip codes that mean nothing to them.

A lot of people who live in the Tompkins Square tent encampment have pets.

Pets are a mental-health boost for everyone; for people living on the streets, they are a lifeline. For many who are single or separated from their families, a dog is their only constant relationship, the only friendship they can count on.

Cynical passersby may assume that the panhandler is "using" a pet for sympathy and that they are subjecting an animal to a life of deprivation, to the point where some consider it acceptable to cut the leashes of an unhoused person's pet while they sleep.

Leslie Irvine wrote a book called *My Dog Always Eats First*, a phrase you will hear time and time again from unhoused people with a mutt pal. In it, she documents stories about how people who live on the streets with pets are drastically less likely to get depressed or engage in risky behaviors than those without an animal friend.

Yet another reason why someone would choose to live in a tent rather than a shelter: most shelters don't allow pets. During excruciating winters or heat advisories, pet owners experiencing homelessness are faced with an impossible dilemma, to drop their pet off at animal control with virtually no chance of seeing them again or to sleep outside. The vast majority choose the latter. When one man interviewed for *My Dog Always Eats First* finally surrendered his dog so that he could regularly go to a shelter, he fell into such a debilitating depression that he relapsed into drug use and couldn't hold a job. Another said that his dog was his main and often only reason to keep living.

Dogs or cats make homelessness bearable, several interviewees agreed. And because of that crucial role, the pets are treated like royalty and prized like walking treasures.

Too frequently, these pet owners don't choose to be separated from their furry friends. During a sweep of the encampments, officials are empowered to take utility blades and slice up tents, tarps, clothes, and sleeping bags. A garbage truck waits nearby to trash all belongings. Food is thrown away, documents are discarded, supplies are trampled.

Then, if there are pets, the officials call animal control or carelessly run off the animals. An individual might return from day labor to find their home destroyed and their beloved companion missing, with no information about how to see them again.

During sweeps, city officials frequently send buses for tent dwellers so they can go to a shelter in an area of town they've never visited. Or they're offered a night in a dingy hotel, then given the number for a system they might bounce around in for years.

"Shelters are safe," you will hear sweep proponents insist time and time again.

No doubt they protect from the elements. But beyond that, whose definition of "safe" are shelters?

They separate men and women, denying the existence of same-sex sexual assault and the possibility of straight married couples who feel uncomfortable sleeping without each other. They ignore the history of safe and well-functioning queer communities comprised of unhoused, rejected, and undervalued human beings who made a family of all genders together. And, like any pet owner is likely to understand, shelter inhabitants don't feel safe without their dog, cat, ferret, or even the usual crew of pigeons.

Tent communities, while far from a solution to a worldwide housing crisis, offer more definitions of safety, and it's no wonder that many folks would prefer tents over shelter beds. To sleep surrounded by possessions, near friends of different genders and species alike, with a door that closes, does seem preferable any day over a bedbug-ridden room of bunks with a strict curfew and a weight limit on belongings.

The outdated definition of "safety" meaning "sterile and separated" takes physical needs into account, but not the soul. Consider a hospital room, far removed from any life existing outside of its walls, outfitted with equipment in that muted pink-beige color that only exists in hospitals. Technically it is safe, but is it good?

Hospitals, prisons, and homeless shelters, in their very design, seem to deny every human's need for one another.

I guess that isn't outrageously surprising, considering how many other ways our culture downplays our interconnectedness, or even just our need for friends. While high school counselors are on hand for career guidance, there aren't any social coaches nudging us to form richer connections and encourage intimacy between peers. In fact, "success" in young adulthood almost always comes back to a competition of some sort—getting ahead of one another to guarantee a future with . . . a 401(k)?

We regard the super wealthy as unbreakably happy people whose money cures all ills. For instance, how often have you heard "Well she's a millionaire, I can't feel sorry for her" or "I'm not going to waste my sympathy on a famous actress." Now how often have you heard "He has a close-knit group of twenty friends who check in on him daily, I can't feel sorry for him."

The latter is key to our happiness and health, and yet woefully undervalued.

I won't romanticize the horror of living on streets and in city parks. In most US cities, it's an actual crime to be unable to pay rent, and it's traumatic to know that your belongings could be taken at any second by people who will likely never be in your position. The wealthy—or even those with stable housing—have the first level of their Maslow's hierarchy of needs checked off. I will say, however, that the tent dwellers I've talked to most often have significant communal values that aren't necessarily a given for folks with higher incomes.

One example: When New York faced a daunting migrant crisis in the wake of two unlivable conflicts in South America and West Africa, the East Village became a hub for thousands from both regions. During a brutal winter, men with families back home lined up every single day for a daily meal promised by the city, distributed at St. Brigid School. Without coats or gloves, and asking strangers for cardboard to sit on, the men would wait for hours only to be handed a Tupperware with moldy bread and an orange.

The city claimed to be overwhelmed with the burden of so many immigrants at once, and the general public vocalized concern that officials would prioritize asylum seekers over citizens. "Why are we feeding illegal immigrants when we can't even take care of our own homeless?" they asked. "What about homeless vets?"

Yet some of the greatest support that New York received in the effort to help asylum seekers came from Americans experiencing homelessness and those who didn't have permanent housing. They didn't want to see other people on the streets. They often had one another's backs. Some of the greatest and most consistent acts of kindness toward migrants came from those who didn't have permanent housing themselves. In Tompkins Square Park, it was an unhoused man who started free English classes at the local community space, and it was a woman in transitional housing who organized a massive food drive to get immigrants fresh produce.

A lot of us buy into the easy narrative that says there isn't enough for everyone, and that makes us feel like if we help A, we can't help B. But those who practice true, real, radical community know that this definition of scarcity is a myth. They also know what it's like to literally ask someone else to save their life. Their lives are saved almost daily by one another.

It's tempting for those who have never entered into such a deep level of intimacy to uphold the thin concept of scarcity, that there's only so much to go around and I need to hoard my share. But those who have been truly desperate—on their knees, at an asking-for-scraps level of desperate—know that to meet another's needs takes nothing from their own.

That winter, I volunteered at a food-and-clothing distribution center for the East Village migrants, and I witnessed the desperation firsthand. I opened a bag of hand warmers and within literal seconds they were ripped out of the bag. The guys from Africa could speak five local languages but not English, and they asked in French for socks.

The other volunteers around me, writing signs in French and Spanish and organizing the soup line, were the same people I'd seen over the summer on the lawn of Tompkins Square Park emerging from tents. A few brought a couple of cans from their own stash, but most just offered some guidance and solidarity—patting backs and writing down phone numbers.

"Love you, love you, love you," said Jimmy, a longtime resident of Tompkins Square Park, as he swerved through the lines of people waiting for sweaters or crackers.

"Love you, man!" shouted back a Mauretanian teenager, who had possibly never said those words in English before.

Humans were not designed to be alone. We don't have stripes that function only for protection in a group, but we've evolved to rely on one another for safety and happiness in this world. We are meant to watch out for one another, to keep one another from harm.

Darwin's theory of survival of the fittest, interestingly enough, came about in tandem with the emergence of capitalism, and the two have been intertwined since. I've examined my own hyperindividualistic instincts through Darwin's lens and thought, *Oh yes, obviously we are hardwired to be skeptical of those who differ from us, to keep ourselves safe!* so I can feel less shame over my own dismissal of those I disagree with. *We were never meant to get along anyway, so how can I be blamed? Look at evolution!*

Well . . . it's not so simple. Darwin helped figure out a lot of much-needed truths about evolution, but he was only one person. A flawed, biased, monumental, complex, imperfect person who had a ton of blind spots, as we all do, and a desired legacy, as we all do.

And while his research generously explained our unflattering but very human desire to compete and see those outside our circle as less valuable than our own kin, he didn't explain how interdependency, resource sharing, community care, and concern for the most vulnerable among us saved our species time and time again.

A zebra herd has a range of nonviolent ways to fight against predators, and every one of them is dependent on being in a group: camouflaging, taking turns, and trading strengths with one another (and ostriches) to thrive as a community.

Likewise, humans in community—especially the flawed ones where we can show up as our raw, imperfect selves—thrive by looking out for one another. That can mean watching belongings while a group member goes to the bathroom or meeting a predator with power in numbers, like the numerous protests that have taken place in Tomkins Square Park since the encampments moved in forty years ago.

I am not entirely anti-zoo, but one of the heartbreaking critiques of animals in any type of captivity is that intergenerational or community bonds are broken when an individual animal is sold or traded to other zoos.

I imagine a young zebra, so codependent on others that she will try to suckle on a moving car and throw herself on the bare leg of a poacher for comfort, being ripped apart from the community she was born to be a part of. The homesickness that must live in her body her whole life is more than any of us understand. She was designed to listen for the warnings of ostriches, blend in with other stripes, stick out her brown tongue in play, and keep watch while a herd member lies down to sleep.

"She's safer in captivity," I will hear from any zoo. "She'll live twenty years longer, she won't have to worry about crocodiles when she drinks water."

But that definition of safety lacks her first protection: a community to take care of her.

And if a tent full of trinkets, birthday cards, a cookie saved for later, a photo labeled MOMMY 1976, a worker's permit, and a beloved plaid coat is thrown in the garbage truck, and its owner is put on a bus to an industrial-warehouse-turned-shelter in a suburb he can't pronounce, it's likely that neither the inhabitant nor his community will feel safe.

Moreover, he will miss out on tomorrow in the park. It's another plump, humid morning, but this time a light breeze is welcoming the second half of summer. Shards of light and laughter and grace will be shared in the park, and one of the church volunteers will come by with a large thermos of coffee and Styrofoam cups.

For all this, the community member won't be here. He will be far away, out of sight, and out of mind from those who never got to know him.

Chapter 8

ON CROCODILES
AND TRUSTING
THE FUTURE

It was the worst day in the history of the planet. First, a blinding flash of light eclipsed the sky. Then, an explosion the equivalent of ten billion nuclear bombs shook the earth. And moments later, the whole world was on fire.

Hot rock and glass rained in a poisonous downpour. Those who survived the first couple of minutes of the asteroid's collision were scorched by unbearable heat. The sky seemed to be caving in as ash from wildfires filled the air above. It was as though the world burned to death, then was buried.

Earlier that day, there had been no warning signs of the coming catastrophe. Earth had experienced a recent wave of global warming that had made the Cretaceous landscape look like a living brochure for a tropical resort. Clear-water creeks murmured down curves of hills overgrown with thriving Technicolor plants to form pools and lakes.

Hours later, those lakes were swallowed whole by a mega-tsunami that tore through the entire continent, flattening forests, flooding canyons, ripping up mountain ranges. And in the following days and weeks, rapid environmental changes made continued life on earth impossible for almost every creature that had thrived until that point.

The blinding flash was the last light the earth would see for a year as ash suffocated the sky in thick, black soot, plunging the world into extended winter. The landscape looked like a postapocalyptic death trap. A layer of earth had burned off and the environment had drastically changed. Most brutally, the dinosaurs went extinct. What took evolution 3.5 billion years to build was destroyed in an instant.

The end of that world was the beginning of ours.

Beneath the charred land, some survivors still slithered and scurried below. They were species who just so happened to have qualities that allowed them to cope. Perhaps, like our rodent-esque ancestors, they didn't rely on living plants for survival but on dead leaves and bark. Or perhaps, like crocodiles, they could go for long stretches without food.

As possibilities for the dinosaur world came to an end, the possibilities for the human world began to emerge. The surviving creatures used the devastation left behind to kindle their own proliferation, learning to grow and adapt with skills to manage this new age. This single worst day in the history of life on earth was as critical for us as it was for the dinosaurs, since it allowed for evolutionary opportunities that had been closed for the previous 165 million years. Mammals could not have developed as they did if dinosaurs had continued.

So the human story really begins at the end of the world. Well, one world.

Our existence doesn't make the end of the dinosaurs any less tragic, but it does help us put the end of their world in context. The world's story isn't life to death in a straight line; it is life, to death, to new life, in a circle.

Each of us has our own individual world, a fragile intricate ecosystem that could be obliterated in a single afternoon. When someone says, "My world is shattered," we get it: what once gave their life meaning is no longer there.

The day after a loss, whether a death or breakup, we may walk around the streets wondering where the beauty went. Suddenly, once-lovely parks and interesting buildings may as well be the scorched remains of the Cretaceous Period. A place that once felt full of life is now empty, offering only fossils.

I don't think it's hyperbolic when we say that our "world has ended" after any sort of loss. A loss shifts who we are and how we understand life. When there's a feeling of "before" and "after" during our lifetime, our day-to-day will never go back to exactly how it was. The world ended. Well, one world.

All this world-ending talk has me thinking about crocodiles. They're one of the few creatures who lived both during and after the dinosaurs. While they were miraculously and uniquely suited to survive an unfathomable apocalypse, they had to evolve at breakneck speed as mammals flourished. They adapted to chase after them and eat them, adding all sorts of delicacies to their diets. And since then, they haven't stopped changing snout and skull shape to fit the climate du jour.

As animals who figure out what to eat as soon as there's a big change, crocodiles are one of evolution's greatest hits. Humans have this in common with them. But we have something more poetic in common with crocodiles when it comes to how we adapt.

The greatest work of any creature is to find new and wondrous possibilities even when it seems that everything has ended. When the asteroid turned planet earth into something unrecognizable, the crocodiles got to work, searching around for what was still there.

Like many people during many world-ending events throughout human history, crocodiles oriented themselves to where they were and what they'd lost.

Then they began to look for signs of new life.

I once took a mosaic class from a physician who had become a ceramic artist after the loss of her two daughters and their father in a plane crash. Years after surveying the charred landscape of her heart for any signs of life, she felt creativity spring deep within and began digging. She rediscovered her childhood love of decorative tiles and followed it to a new career as an art therapist who helps grieving people make memorial mosaics for their loved ones.

When we are shocked by loss, when our world seemingly crumbles in an instant, turning toward creation is intuitive. What new existence can come out of this loss? It is up to us to answer that question.

"Beginnings need endings, a lesson that we can either hold carefully or that we can deny until it finds us." So writes Riley Black, author of *The Last Days of the Dinosaurs*, a book about the great extinction of dinosaurs as an important moment in the history of humans: both because it's how we began and it's likely how we will end.

How could anyone have believed that the glorious world of dinosaurs, that the powerful empire of Rome, that a sweet first love, would ever end? How many worlds will end during this planet's lifespan, and what will come next?

At the end of the musical *Hadestown*, based on the tragic Greek love story between Orpheus and Eurydice, the narrator sings a melancholy anthem as Eurydice is forever banished beneath the earth. He recounts the tale, then promises to keep telling it again, as though maybe next time will be different. Of course it never is, but he'll keep telling it even so.

And the next day at tomorrow's performance, the Broadway cast will literally sing the story again, the Greek myth repeating itself over and over, as myths always do.

The myths remind us that we're not special. We're no more exquisite than the dinosaurs, no more powerful than the Romans, and our love is fragile too. Our world will also fall. Maybe yours already has. Mine's fallen a few times.

But here's one more thing we have in common with crocodiles:

we know how to look for new life after death. We ourselves are the living silver linings of a former earth we can only begin to imagine, one that had to end so we could start.

It's why people still seek healthy relationships after being cheated on or keep submitting their writing for publication after months of rejection. Even the most jaded among us will still keep an eye out for the life that we know must be there, even if we have to create it ourselves.

Perhaps we won't survive the next catastrophe; perhaps we just don't happen to have the qualities for it. Many people are certain that we're living in the end times, and that very well might be true. But end times always give way to new beginning times.

If we could build our civilizations over molten ash, if we could reinstill trust in our broken hearts, if we could keep knocking on doors even after one hundred rejections, then we can believe there will be an "and" following whatever world ends next.

Crocodiles have an eternal "and" built into their ancient DNA; humans have to work a little harder at hope. But by observing what these powerful reptiles have been through and how often they've adapted themselves as a different world emerged, perhaps we can learn what we too are capable of surviving.

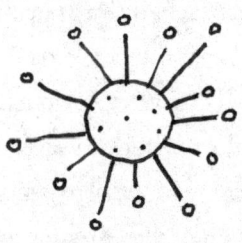

Chapter 9

ON CHICKENS
AND LEARNING
NEW LANGUAGES

To tell you the truth, I don't think about chickens very much.

In the grand scheme of things that occupy my mind, including beings from the animal world, chickens are appallingly low on the list.

So when I woke up early to go spend some alone time with the famed donkeys who live at the retreat center where I write, I was irritated when the farmhand, a spectacularly disheveled man so rough around the edges and yet so eager that he could have been either twenty-five or forty-five years old, stopped me to tell me about the chickens.

It was apparently their morning social hour and they had all congregated between me and the donkey pen. Gary kept adjusting his baseball cap as he proudly announced, "Hey, you're just in time to meet the chickens."

This was very much something I had no interest in doing, but unfortunately, I was at a retreat center whose mission includes promoting peace between all living beings so I couldn't very well charge through the chickens to get to the far more fascinating donkeys.

I just smiled and feigned affection. "Ohhh, cute!"

Gary was placated and began a slow yet continuous ramble about the personalities, breeds, and behaviors of each chicken, all while holding and stroking a black hen in the crook of his elbow who looked as mild and sleepy as a house cat.

I tuned out, my eyes darting toward the donkeys, until he got to the black hen. "This is my baby, Edna. You can tell she's relaxed because she's looking around; she's not focusing. She loves to be pet."

I was surprised at his tenderness. I'd seen him around the farm earlier carrying a bundle of tools under one arm and a sack of compost in the other. I didn't associate those practical arms with ones that could also rock a chicken to sleep.

I shifted my attention away from the donkeys and more fully on what Gary was saying.

"So Edna's the sweetest one . . . then there's Tuck, the rooster. He's a big baby. And that one climbing up on you is Dog. Because she acts like a dog."

Dog the chicken was a gorgeous blond, a strawberry-lemonade hue that models in Manhattan would die for. Dog lightly pecked my arm, no doubt looking for food, then settled on my thigh. As Gary told me about her breed, her eyes would slowly close and quickly reopen, just like everyone's grandpa as he falls asleep to the evening news.

The chickens began making noises, but they didn't sound like any of the *Buk buk buk buk ba-gawk!* sounds I'd heard in cartoons or from stuffed animal chickens that make a noise when you pull a cord.

Rather, their sounds were sweet and soft, reminding me a lot of my cat when she's purring too loud to formulate a robust *meow* and settles for huffs and whispered chirps instead. I thought about how heavenly it would be to hear these sounds every morning, the world's most pleasant alarm clock.

"They're talking to each other," said Gary, who I was now fully convinced was an enlightened being. As he stretched and squinted his eyes toward the mountains, he went on. "Yeah they talk to each other when they think there's a threat, like, *Guys let's get out of here.* Sometimes they're reminding each other of their social structure, like, *Hey remember I'm in charge*, or just expressing joy or fear, and sometimes, who knows what they're talking about. Right now they're chatting about where the food is."

He emitted a chortle and kept petting Edna.

Gary finally left for the next chore of the day, which apparently involved a shovel, and I was free to commune with the donkeys. But I kept looking back at the chickens.

The next afternoon, I went to revisit the donkeys and noticed the community of hens and one kingly rooster pecking around in front of them again. This time, no Gary.

As I walked down the grassy slope toward the pen, I saw one white hen look up at me (I had forgotten her name). She released an impressive *peeeeep,* and suddenly, the entire flock began walking in my direction. It's a comical sight to watch chickens try to hurry; their angular feet extend from their soft, fluffy bodies in military fashion, as though they were two separate animals smooshed together.

For a brief moment, I had about fifty chickens rushing (as much as a chicken can rush) toward me, emitting peeps and chirps and other sorts of squeals we normally associate with chihuahuas.

It was heaven.

I'm certain they were trading rumors around that I had food—after all, Gary had poured me a handful of treats to feed them yesterday—but no matter. For a brand-new chicken appreciator, it was like having fifty golden retrievers smiling and tail-wagging at me for merely being alive.

Their clucks are what really got me; they all chattered incessantly. I was so curious what they must have been talking about. I noticed some particularly gossipy chickens clucking the most often and the loudest, and others hanging out in the back, simply eavesdropping. (I've found that the ones in the back are often the finest tattletales.)

I made my way toward the donkeys but couldn't get these clucks, chirps, peeps, and downright barks off my mind. Why hadn't I heard about chicken language? I'd been obsessing over animals—especially the ones we eat!—for years now, and not once had I stumbled upon the wide world of chicken lingo.

That evening, I looked up "chicken language" online. Maybe I should have known that I would get all kinds of bizarre results and very few about actual transmissions between chickens.

Huh, I thought. *That's weird. They are so vocal!*

Then I deleted "language" and replaced it with "communication."

"How do chickens communicate?"

Now, thousands of results.

I chortled like Gary.

Ohhhhh, I realized. *We don't call animal sounds "language." We reserve that for humans.*

We know that parrots communicate with one another verbally, yet we don't call it "language." Meanwhile, parrots can mimic many human words and understand and use them correctly, and we humans have not managed to speak a single word of any parrot language.

I was astounded that Gary could interpret the squawks and purrs of hens but frustrated when the birds seemingly couldn't decipher the difference between my commands of "Eat" and "Wait." I'm enamored with any animal whisperer who can tell horses that they're safe or urge feral tabbies to be less violent, yet I've never marveled at the fact that my own cat knows her human name (one of several!) or that the street dogs of San Miguel de Allende are so accustomed to tourists that they obey "Sit" in three different languages.

It's so easy to believe humans have language, animals have communication. But what, really, is the difference? Language is intricate, yes, but I need months of lessons to get by in Russia within my own species. Chickens, on the other hand, can welcome in a new member from a foreign flock and make it work.

When I listen to chickens clearly talk to one another, I reflect on all the languages I have spoken in my life. I don't mean foreign languages—the ones I learned in school—but the ones I learned through experience.

When I lived in Washington, DC, I felt like everyone had their life together except for me. Depending on one's subculture, DC can seem like a city oriented toward the linear success of traditional careers—the ones that provide insurance and involve standing desks and pencil skirts and "circling back on this."

I had no such thing. I took refuge in the words of author Cheryl Strayed: "You don't have a career. You have a life."

But lives don't pay rent. Nor do they have much to say for themselves at dinner parties when someone dutifully asks, "What do you do?" in the same tone that one might ask, "Why are you worth my time?"

"I work at a store, I want to be a writer, I do yoga, and I cook myself a fabulous dinner every night," my friend advised me to reply with my chin held high.

Yet at some point I just decided to stop being in situations where I'd be surrounded by Career Talk; it was eroding my self-worth to be on the defense about my unplanned, uninsured life.

That's when I discovered the world of Going Out Dancing.

I thought Going Out Dancing was a phase of life that I had already missed, or something that happened in foreign countries, or a weekend activity for people who had completely different personalities from mine.

Turns out, it was available for me too, and I started doing it a few times a week. I quickly began learning all sorts of new languages: the names of DJs, the origins of song samples, the distinct vibe of each club.

Obviously, I was safe from Career Talk at the clubs. It wasn't just that my fellow Tuesday-night Go-Out-Dancers weren't interested in day jobs; the language of it literally didn't exist in this culture, a culture that was *also* very much at home in DC (the birthplace of several subgenres of hip-hop, funk, soul, and punk).

While those Career People had the days of DC, we had the nights.

I began to reframe my insecurity around career-track conversations: there wasn't anything wrong with my life; I was just uncomfortable with a language I didn't know. (Flashbacks to my host family in Kobe talking over each other in Japanese during dinner while I sat there wondering if I could slide under the table without them noticing.)

Once I mastered the language of dance music, I became okay with not having a fancy career because I had something else that I cherished so much more. I picked up other tongues too: those of the local art community, my samba lessons, the trails of Rock Creek Park.

Now that I had fluency elsewhere in cultures that felt more like home, I could sit among the career gibberish and just smile, knowing that I didn't have to understand or contribute much. I was going out dancing later. I'd be able to talk up a storm with no accent in the local language I knew best.

There are plenty of times when I'm speaking English to someone—quite clearly, I might add—and they are speaking English to me—with equal clarity, I'll concede—and it feels like we're speaking two different languages. When I meet someone and we instantly click, I say, "You speak my language."

We're using the same word—"language"—to mean different things. How beautiful it is that any one human can speak so many languages of different kinds: a native Portuguese speaker can also communicate in the language of baking, São Paulo's coffee culture, their extended family's particularities, street cats, and computer science.

The problem is when it seems like the world values some languages more highly than others. Meanwhile, isn't it so cool that we're all polyglots in our own way? Wouldn't life become infinitely richer if we could all channel our inner Gary and learn a devalued language like that of chickens?

During those excruciating DC happy hours years ago, I'd think, *I just don't speak this language.* That there's nothing wrong with me and nothing wrong with them either (because we all know how quickly insecurity transforms into judgment). *I just speak a different language.* But as much as I told myself that, I often got discouraged when I didn't speak the "right" tongue.

It would take me many more years, journeys, and life experiences—not to mention encounters with chickens!—to truly believe that each language is as valid as the next. While I never fully regarded my fluency in Going Out Dancing as highly as my friends' in Talking About Insurance, I gained confidence once I started adding a few more vernaculars to my repertoire.

As soon as I arrived in Panama City last spring, I was reminded of one of my highest levels in the Duolingo of life: I am *very* good at being in a foreign country. I can identify the nonscammer in the taxi line and confidently negotiate a rate, I can elbow my way out of prickly situations, I can make friends through charades, and I can always find a bathroom no matter what.

I was telling my fellow nomadic Spanish teacher about this and she replied, "See, it doesn't matter that you can't do your taxes! You're good at other things!"

SHE'S RIGHT!

(It actually does matter that I can't do my taxes. But she's still right.)

I have this one specific skill that barely ever comes up in my normal life, but I'm really, really good at it! I may not speak the language of a W-9 form but I *do* speak the language of figuring out how to walk across a multilane highway in Panama City, and let me tell you, it is an Everest-level accomplishment!

I used to walk into dance clubs in DC and feel an instant sense of proud belonging: *I know what I'm doing here.* I had the uniform, I understood the space, I knew the dances, I got the culture, I spoke the language. At those parties full of professionals, I felt as important and intelligent as a piece of sock lint, but at the club I could shine. Or at least my sequin jacket could shine.

Now I feel that way about other places. I could probably walk into most yoga studios and feel comfortable (except for that one in Lower Manhattan . . .).

I'm better at public speaking than public most-other-things and I feel relaxed when I walk onstage. In the application for my chaplaincy internship, I wrote that I'm not anxious walking into a hospital and have no problem talking about death (the only qualification I could bring to the table, but it seemed like an important one). And I'm pleased to announce that I finally don't feel overwhelmed when I walk through the spice aisle of the grocery store.

Thinking in terms of the life languages I speak and the ones I simply don't (e.g., sports isn't happening in this lifetime) helps me smooth out my insecurities.

I remember that as I envision the spaces I still don't feel comfortable walking into but would someday like to. Maybe I can try venturing into tax prepping and professional mingling and sports chatting and all the many worlds where I don't feel welcome simply by approaching them with an open "I know just a couple phrases" mentality.

Despite the internet's shortening of our physical distances, the world still holds an inexhaustible amount of actual languages and thus an inexhaustible amount of ways for people to legitimately express themselves. Every language has syllables and sounds that are nearly impossible for nonnative speakers to mimic but so enjoyably challenging to try.

There are always spaces and languages that may seem out of reach. But there's also no shortage of ways to get comfortable in this world if you're willing to look around.

My linguistic skills have changed over time; I can only remember a few basic words now from Going Out Dancing. But I'm steadily incorporating other ones from the languages of Nature World, Cooking World, Living-Joyfully-in-Grief World, and I'm dabbling in others to feel more at home on this oddball, glorious earth.

The chickens who gather in front of the donkey pen have come to feel at home on this oddball, glorious earth—a place whose dominant species doesn't highly prize the noble chicken—by developing an exuberant symphony of peeps and chirps. It's a full, layered language that I can only appreciate on a surface level—much like the language of accountants or people who can easily wake up before dawn without large buckets of coffee.

While I don't presume I'll speak fluent Chicken in this lifetime, I now know that they have a language that exists! Maybe like Gary,

I'll learn enough to be able to step in and out of their private world as long as they'll have me, but I'll always be a visitor.

In hindsight, I was only a temporary resident in the world of Going Out Dancing, but learning the language taught me that I could belong somewhere, and that particular somewhere mattered to a lot of people. I wasn't a less valuable human for not having a particular job; it's just that my particular city seemed to value one job's language a little more.

Some of my most exhilarating moments in DC were when I'd invite a friend to my Going Out Dancing World and quickly realize she didn't speak even the basic phrases. It wasn't that I was smug (okay, I was smug), but her speechlessness reminded me that I had learned a language well enough to translate. As fancy as her job was, I could still offer her my own skills, equally valuable.

If you ever begin feeling dangerously close to thinking you know everything, hang out in a group where you don't speak the language. You will be awakened to new forms of intelligence and a grounding sense of humility—in this group, you're the novice.

Greatly outnumbered by chickens, I was not the dominant species. And I know it would take a few lifetimes to understand the chatter between them: Are there jokes? Stories? Laments? Attempts to tell us how to treat them? All I know for sure is I'll be thinking about chickens for a long time.

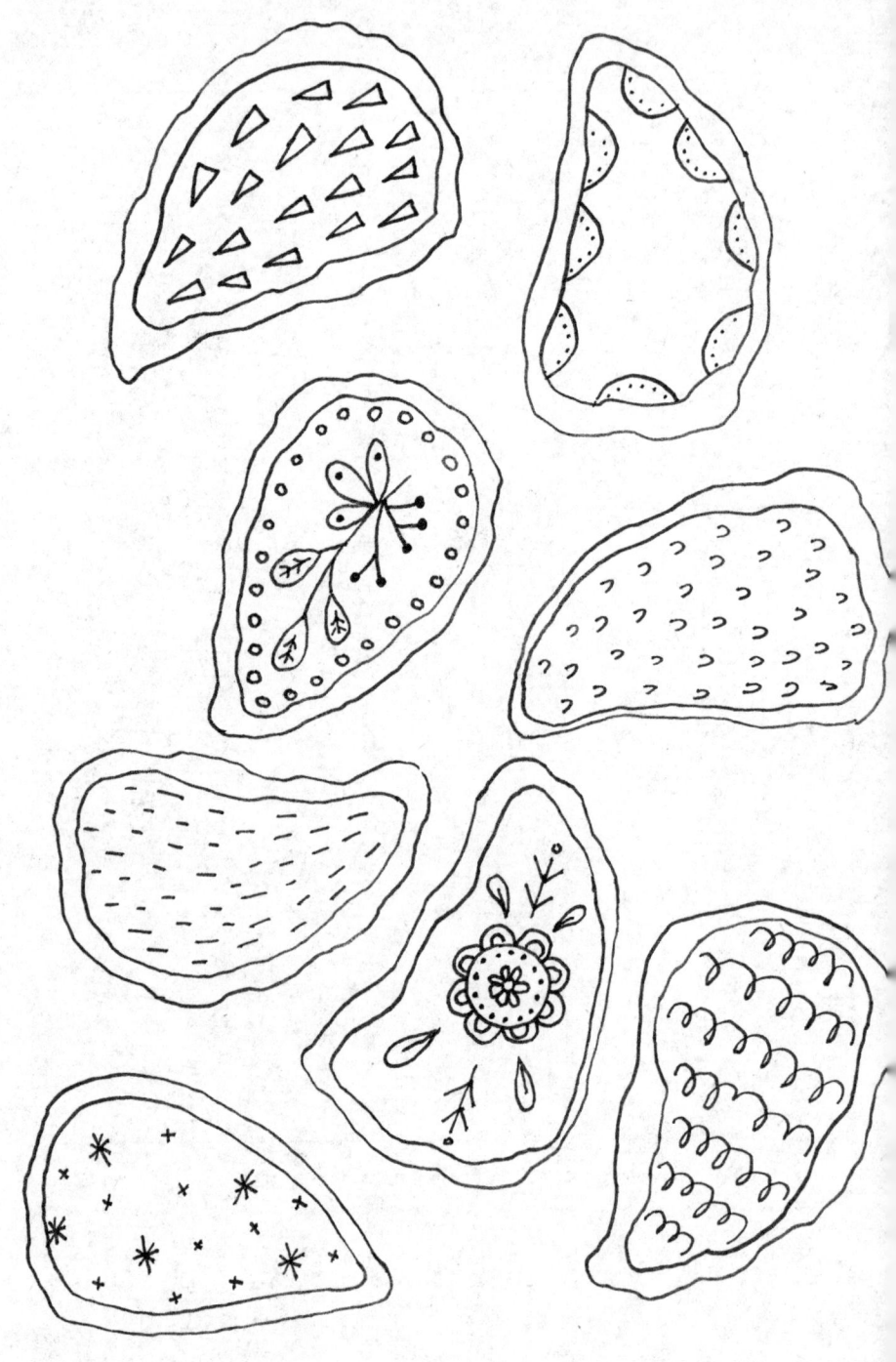

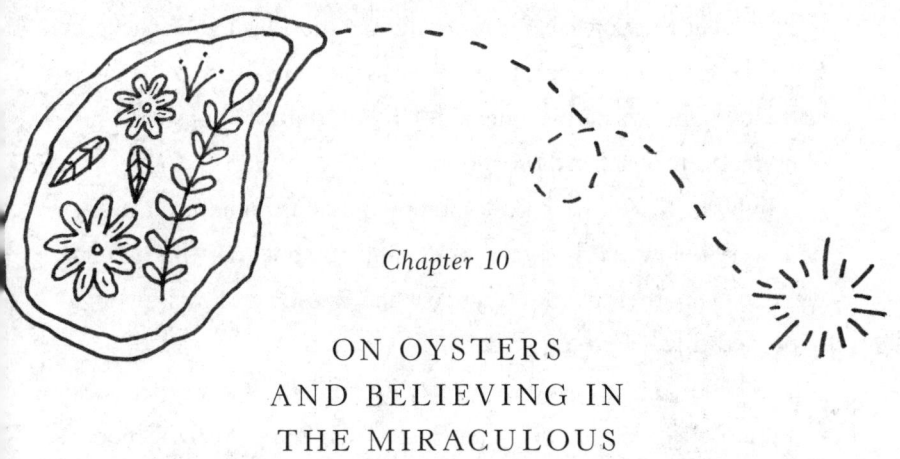

Chapter 10

ON OYSTERS
AND BELIEVING IN
THE MIRACULOUS

I recently read an article about displaced oysters. These poor tykes grew up on the damp, textured beaches of Connecticut but were taken mid-life to the golden fields of the prairie by a scientist named Frank Brown.

Frank had a keen fascination with mollusks. He kept them in a darkroom three hours north of Chicago and studied them attentively day and night.

Frank knew that oysters are most active during the two high tides of the day, which is when the water becomes an all-you-can-eat plankton buffet, and he wanted to see what they would do if they were hundreds of miles from the nearest sea.

For the first couple of weeks, their feeding schedule kept time with their home beach in New Haven. Turns out you can't take the Nathan Hale Beach out of the oyster, or however that saying goes.

But what the homesick critters did next left him gobsmacked. Over the following weeks, they adjusted their mealtime to be later and later. This was a big puzzle for Frank until he consulted his almanac and considered the moon.

High tides occur each day when the moon is highest in the sky or lowest below the horizon. Frank figured out that the oysters were enjoying their plankton binge when Evanston, Illinois, would hypothetically have a high tide.

Locked in a Midwest darkroom with no light or any other cues from the outside world, the oysters were still in touch with the moon.

Frank was elated to share this news, but he was met by critics who wanted his work scrubbed out of their field for not being "scientific enough." His colleagues weren't as open as he was to the perceptive abilities of other creatures; their field was a product of the Enlightenment, where rationality ruled and everything else was baloney. Frank became the butt of a joke about what happens when you stray from common sense. "You know the guy who thinks oysters get signals from the sky?"

But our friend Frank doubled down! He began studying the metabolic rate of potatoes, which, despite being isolated from their farms of origin, could also clearly sense the hour of the day and season of the year.

He eventually claimed that all living things must be sensitive to all kinds of signals, even forces that hadn't been discovered yet by humans. Life was pulsing in time with earth, and all its organisms were bathed in subtle rhythms while the planet spun.

Though Frank's evidence was concrete, he joined the legions of mystics, visionaries, prophets, intuitive empaths, shamans, medicine women, revolutionaries, sensitive souls, and anyone with a special connection to the land and animals, whose ideas have been laughed at and dismissed throughout history.

While I don't assume Frank was exactly a flower child, it *was* a radical claim that oysters could sense something beyond the secured tubs of a dingy underground lab and—likely much more threatening—that humans *weren't* able to sense it.

How dare a scientist hint that the world's wonders are not necessarily explicable and may not even be *perceptible* to human beings?! By insinuating such, Frank practically committed blasphemy against Reason.

Decades later, nobody knows what to make of these calcified invertebrates and their moon-sensing magic. Because oysters must be so highly attuned to something we can't perceive, we may never fully understand it.

An interesting thing happened in my dance class the other day.

I've immersed myself in dance this year—sort of accidentally. While joining a friend at hip-hop aerobics, I remembered a joyful feeling that had lain dormant in my soul since the last jazz class I took twenty years ago. Now I go to four classes a week, and I'm often the oldest, usually the worst, and *always* the smiliest participant. Dancing gives me a feeling I can't explain, but if pressed, I'd say it has something to do with expressing a part of myself that never gets released in daily life.

As of late, I've used dancing to express emotions that don't naturally slip into the spaces society has carved out for feelings. This last year, I've been fiddling with several Rubik's Cubes of complicated grief. I'm grieving my beloved stepdad whose loss can't feel like mine as long as people ask, "How's your mom doing?" but never ask about me. I'm mourning the death of a friend who struggled with depression for years—even though we hadn't talked during all those years. I'm growing apart from a close relative and out of some beliefs I've been attached to for years.

These puzzles prick me with pain all day long, but they're not easy to describe. *Sorry I didn't get back to your email, I was lying on the floor in a starfish position thinking about a Facebook status my dead friend wrote seven years ago, and it really put me in a funk.*

So, instead of explaining my feelings, I dance my feelings. I dance out grief, grace, survivor's guilt, giddiness, resentment, and everyday annoyance. More often than not, I pry myself out of a crowded subway and stumble into class announcing, "I want to scream at everyone!" By the end of class, I'm euphoric enough to consider high-fiving everyone.

The other day, a neurologist came to class. Inspired by some articles suggesting that dance could be a treatment modality for some mental disorders, she observed our moods and took furious notes throughout class.

I wasn't surprised because, of course. *Of course* dance is a treatment modality. *Of course* dance improves our mood. *Of course* it fosters connection, tightens community, metabolizes emotion, releases stress, increases confidence, etc. etc. etc. etc. We've only been doing this for hundreds of thousands of years.

The need to study and *prove* the benefits of dance amused me. I wanted to tell the neurologist, "Why don't you just try it . . . okay, there, that's your proof!"

It also made me a bit sad. There are so many exciting phenomena on this gloriously strange planet we've found ourselves upon, and so many of them is knowable if we choose to accept that there are many different ways to know something.

From the deepest part of me—the part that feels connected to chanting ancestors in a Nordic forest that I will never visit, the part that wails in grief when I don't care who hears it—I know dance is healing me. I don't need to appease my finicky brain with studies and statistics and proof. I feel it in my feet, and that is enough.

I also don't need written proof that there is aliveness in rocks and water, or that trees have families, or that animals care for one another. I know all that.

The things I've "known" in this particular way—in my belly, as though I was born knowing them—have served me the most. The things I've learned with my mind? They're the ones that change over time and most often disappoint me.

The neurologist at my dance class reminded me of how I will often seek evidence that something is, in fact, good for me even when it *feels* good for me. More energy, better sleep, and sustained vibrancy isn't enough. I'm over here googling "Is a plant-based diet better for you?" I'm willing to give away my own power of intuition the minute I get on my keyboard in order to fact-check my own instinct.

I wonder if this is what Frank Brown was up against when his fellow biologists were mad at him for noticing that oysters boast a strong relationship with the moon. Why would this be so astounding in a world with lavender skies, green-sand beaches, hundred-pound rocks that sail across deserts, a volcano that burns blue, and another that erupts with ice?

For some of the wildest and most beautiful phenomena in the world, the scientific explanation is *inconclusive*. Yet somehow we understand it all from the ancient depths of our bellies.

I learned a word for this: "transrational." It means "going beyond or surpassing human reason."

Modern Western science would likely teach that irrationality is the opposite of rationality. But what if they weren't opposites? What if modern science was expansive enough to hold the idea that there are wonders and miracles and oyster habits that go beyond what we can comprehend in a science-y way and yet we can still believe them?

Take "love" for instance. Can anyone define it? Greek philosophers and fifties teenage crooners alike have tried, and it all comes out sounding pretty corny, even trite. There is no scientific explanation of love that anyone can agree on. My definition may vary from yours or from Whitney Houston's or John Keats's, but it doesn't matter. The world seems to intuitively agree that love doesn't need to be delineated to be understood.

Robin Wall Kimmerer, botanist and member of the Citizen

Potawatomi Nation, points out that science refines the gift of seeing, quite literally through various lenses like the magnifying glass or microscope. But science looks only at the *material* being.

In contrast, she says, "In Indigenous ways of knowing, we say that we know a thing when we know it not only with our physical senses, with our intellect, but *also* when we engage our intuitive ways of knowing—of emotional knowledge and spiritual knowledge." Rather than *looking*, traditional knowledge teaches us to *listen*.

When I think of listening in order to understand, I imagine my entire body orienting toward the subject at hand: a bed of moss, a ladybug, a high tide filled with feasting oysters.

I listen with my belly, with my teeth, with my knees, and with every cell of mine that can perceive. I remind my brain to take a rest and withhold the commentary. And sometimes after a couple minutes, sometimes after years, the "knowing" comes so easily:

Of course oysters can feel the pull of the moon, even from a landlocked darkroom. If I listen long enough, it's so logical that I'd be surprised if it *weren't* the case.

Of course dung beetles navigate using the stars; they roll their dung balls along straight paths under starlit skies—but not in overcast conditions.

Of course termites use their heads to drum in order to signal danger to other termites. As soon as they perceive a threat, they begin, and those who hear the drumming also start drumming so as to help warn as many termites as possible.

Of course orangutans have the wisdom to self-medicate with what's available to them. When wounded Sumatran orangutans make a paste from a native plant known to locals as having healing properties and chew the leaves for good measure. Is this intuition, learned behavior, evolution, or spiritual inkling? Does it matter?

Notice how you never come across a study that concludes, "Animals are actually stupider than we think!" The more seekers of all kinds of knowledge (poets and scientists alike!) investigate the inner world of nonhuman creatures, the more magical we realize they are.

I've noticed an abrupt change in my thinking during the past couple of years. While I could once feel the firm grasp of my mind on her many opinions—as rigid and unchanging as rock formations on the beach—my brain seems to have loosened up. My whole body feels looser (for better or worse), and I can sense more spaciousness within me. There is a lot more space for contradictions, conflicting ideas, and fresh questions to old answers.

Some days, it's exciting: my mind's eye is watching a minimalist black-and-white painting become smudged into finger-painted gray. With so much streaky uncertainty, I feel younger than I did fifteen years ago when I knew I was right about everything.

Other days, my identity is shaky without such strong feelings propping it up. Unwavering morals that once led me to boycott, ban, and boast about my behavior now flex and stretch beyond recognition.

I find myself shrugging a lot more. And answering, "That seems true." And saying the exact same thing to the opposing argument.

Rather than my beliefs becoming sharper and more finessed, they've become rather dull. I've found myself concerned about my apparent apathy and disinterest in picking fights.

On the flip side, I'm an easier person to be around. I don't cut people off because they have different recycling habits. I feel a lot calmer, while simultaneously being more curious. I like inhabiting a more spacious self.

When I consider Robin Wall Kimmerer's broad definition of "knowledge" as both seeing and listening, I imagine my life gently divided into two halves: the first, intent on seeing; the second, devoted to listening.

Young people are blessed with the passionate drive to see. They notice everything, and name their observations plainly, without hesitation. They show our world to us. Sometimes our eyes become too groggy, even crusted over, so that we are no longer really *looking* at the world but rather just passing through it. Young people alert us to what's wrong.

But maybe the sense I'm honing as I get older is listening. Listening lets me in on a different way of knowing, one that isn't intent on concluding as much as it is on simply experiencing.

When I experience the sensation of dance, I'm open to its magical transformative powers, powers that defy vocabulary. While experiencing an encounter with an animal, I'm open to its sacredness. At dinner with a friend, I'm open to this sliver of his life and his vast mind and the comingling of our beliefs.

The priest Richard Rohr talks about living with lightness and inner freedom in the second half of life. He writes that the universe has the opportunity to surprise and enchant us once we give up control. As we grow up and age, we realize that we could never *plan* for joy; it only comes through spaces we leave when our life is loose enough to notice it in the first place.

We learn over time that planning the perfect party is often a bust, and the best times are usually unexpected. In a loose life, nothing can be held too tightly—neither plan nor perspective. It's only then when a person is able to press their ear against the heartbeat of their life and listen with full intention.

Any time I am ambivalent about loosening my grip on so many strongly held convictions of my more radical youth, I recall oyster enthusiast Frank Brown and soften toward acceptance.

Because of his spacious mind and loose life, he was completely open to the idea that mollusks would track the moon's movements even when it seemed—given human limitations—impossible to do so.

Impossible, sure, but they were doing it! This clearly delighted Frank, as he kept listening to all kinds of beings across a range of aliveness throughout his career, even while his colleagues thought his spacious imagination—and all the magical findings he entertained—didn't belong in science.

If growing older means becoming looser and more spacious in our thinking, perhaps science is also becoming roomier. People like Robin Wall Kimmerer invite us to expand how we even define knowledge, as do so many other biologists from backgrounds that Western scientific fields have too long ignored or overlooked.

Funny how maturity so often looks like returning to childhood, when possibilities were so much bigger than they ever are again. Little kids don't separate subjects into clean spaces on a school schedule: *this* is fact, *this* is poetry, *this* is spirituality.

Instead, they, like Frank, see it all as the same—unnecessarily separated by textbooks and experts. Why can't philosophy belong in math, which can belong in literature, which can belong in biology, which can belong in what used to be called "sorcery"? There are as many ways to perceive the world as there are beings on this world. We won't be privy to them all in this lifetime, but we can start by loosening our lives. It doesn't have to happen dramatically all at once, of course. It can be just a bit here and there. A roomier conjecture. A more spacious opinion. Just enough expanse to think about considering the fact that an oyster can perceive the gravity of the moon. Just that. And then, with all that extra free space to wiggle around in science, philosophy, and magic, who knows what we'll discover?

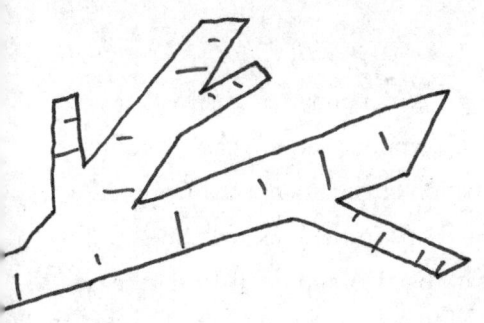

Chapter 11

ON CARDINALS
AND CREATING YOUR
OWN HOLINESS

Easter is my favorite holiday, especially in the city—a pastel panoply of bread bunnies in the windows of Italian bakeries, flower garlands draped across streetlights, and extravagant hats parading down Fifth Avenue on a warm, pastoral morning. It was also the first holiday I had to figure out how to observe during the pandemic lockdown in New York City.

I wanted to celebrate it but I felt silly, like anything I did would be playing pretend and thus require some buy-in from my own mind.

Easter often falls on one of the first warm, sunny days of the year after a brutal Northeast winter, and 2020 was no exception. The magnolia tree outside my house was putting on quite the show with its brand-new blush blossoms; in fact, the whole block looked like a red-carpet fashion show of different colors and shapes.

The flowers were celebrating spring no matter what, whereas I was having a philosophical crisis about how to mark a holiday without the communal participation of ritual—not to mention the ability to pick up a package of Peeps in the checkout line at the supermarket. While the days ran together and the calendar began to feel eerily meaningless, I thought way too much about how holidays are constructs and there is no real reason why one day should differ from another. And still I experienced the human drive to make meaning.

My Easter meaning-making experiment involved ordering a lavish Easter-feast box from a local restaurant, which I gobbled while watching a church service online. Then I "hunted" for chocolate eggs that I hid from myself a day before. I dressed up, even though no one would see me. To be honest, it all felt very strange.

But after a while, as more pandemic-era holidays passed, I got the hang of consecrating the ordinary. I watched others excel at it. Two of my friends got married while sitting on a couch and e-signing the certificate, then drank the most meaningful twelve-dollar prosecco of their lives. Another friend's parents took out "the good china" once a week to mark Friday evening, complete with a cheese plate. It was just serving ware and a block of Havarti, but with attention and the intentional use of a joy-giving ceremony, those objects transformed into set-apart sacraments.

I saw more cardinals than I ever had in my life during the muddy spring of the early pandemic, when I took long walks to fill those daunting afternoons that seemed to stretch the day well past twenty-four hours. I'd gasp after seeing a streak of red in the sky. Had these beautiful cardinals been here all this time? Why hadn't I noticed them before?

That spring, what I once considered sacred was flipped upside down. Places of worship closed and gatherings were forbidden, so any ordinary materials that were normally transformed by ritual—bread, oil, Sabbath candles, and palm fronds—were just objects. Exclusive restaurants that normally had a monthslong waiting list became awkwardly accessible, serving wildly pricey entrées in Styrofoam take-out containers.

This big flip liberated a lot of us to decide what was sacred for *ourselves*. Emptied churches and reconfigured traditions gave everyday folks the opportunity to take the "holy" out of priests' hands or temple walls and bring it into the world.

The word "cardinal" came from the Latin *cardinalis*, meaning "hinge" and later arose to mean "chief, essential," as in, "The fate of the Catholic Church hinges on the decision-making skills of the cardinals!" Cardinals in Catholicism were the bigwigs, and their name's etymology reflects their tremendous importance in the Middle Ages.

At that particular moment in church history, plenty of monks and theologians insisted that the material world was created directly by God, and thus is fundamentally connected with God's goodness.

But the church leaders themselves—the most powerful men at

the time—were not so convinced. If normal laypeople could know God through their senses while communing with nature, then what good was the hierarchal church?

This ego fragility is why I'm amused by the fact that those men in power—the VIPs of the megainfluential church—accidentally influenced the naming of a bird. A lowly, ordinary *bird*!

A century later, Pilgrims who were still fighting off scurvy in the name of their own religious freedom began giving English names to all the American creatures they'd never seen before. Indigenous tribes throughout the land had their own words for this scarlet critter: the Ojibwe called them "misko-bineshiinh" and the Cherokee called them "totsuhwa." The Cherokee in particular treasured them as carriers of news, both good and bad.

But the Puritans were focused on the remarkable color; they called the red-feathered friend a "cardinal" after the bright red outfits worn by officials in the Catholic Church, a force that persecuted them before they left.

Religion tells us what's sacred and what isn't, but art and literature merge that duality into one concept. So I bet it was an artsy writer in the Pilgrim group who made the connection between the red capes of the church cardinals and the red feathers of the bird who elicited delight in the middle of a grueling first winter on Massachusetts shores.

As Polish poet Wisława Szymborska put it, "In daily speech, where we don't stop to consider every word, we all use phrases like 'the ordinary world,' 'ordinary life,' 'the ordinary course of events.' . . . But in the language of poetry, where every word is weighed, nothing is usual or normal. Not a single stone and not a single cloud above it. Not a single day and not a single night after it. And above all, not a single existence, not anyone's existence in this world."

While in Europe, church officials had final say on what was holy and what was unholy; the Pilgrims who were free of the church's tight grip could now consecrate various objects or animals for themselves.

The Pilgrims might have seen the cardinal as sacred, as the Cherokee do. Cardinals don't migrate like so many other birds; they remain steadfast through the winter, committed to their home even during its harshest season. While humans are tempted from time to time to escape our lives when they are less than ideal, the cardinal stays devoted, resilient through all seasons.

Perhaps cardinals were a special symbol to the English Puritans who couldn't leave the brutal Northeast winter for a Florida beach. Cardinals certainly became sacred to me when I stayed in New York through the seasons of a tough year. How I wanted to run away from the city—run away from my own life!—but watching those loyal cardinals anchored me at home.

The historic definition of "holy" is "set apart." A holy thing is something that is set apart from the ordinary or common. Lockdown erased those lines and turned meaning inside out. A cappuccino from a coffee shop became the most covetable, special substance in the world, while Communion wine sat in bottles in church basements—just fermented grape juice. People staying at home had to decide for themselves how much emphasis they would put on holidays that seemed arbitrary when everything that was set apart or unavailable to us—grocery shopping, gathering in a cramped apartment, sharing dessert—were the things that used to be the most ordinary of all.

If you think about what makes an object holy in a religious setting, it's ultimately attention and intentional use. Bread is just a sandwich ingredient until a priest holds it up, breaks it in half, and feeds us one by one. A couple of leaves of romaine lettuce can be a treat for your pet hamster or a base for Caesar salad until the Passover seder begins, and then they're a reminder of the bitterness of the Israelites' enslavement. A waxy apple from the grocery store, sticker label hopelessly affixed, becomes an offering to the ancestors on a Hindu altar or Day of the Dead ofrenda.

During those early lockdown days, my friends and I wanted to believe that we'd never take the ordinary for granted again. We fantasized about sitting down at a restaurant, having our vision blocked by a tall person at a concert, or grocery shopping without lining up outside.

"I'll never, ever cancel plans to a party again!" I declared.

But human adaptability is an astounding mechanism. We somehow got used to wearing masks over our faces, and then, when we reemerged from the worst of lockdown, we just as quickly got used to sitting in coffee shops and grumbling that the supermarket was out of our brand of peanut butter.

Once again, the sacred got all blurry. Rather than an indulgent (and potentially risky!) treat, a latte was just a latte. While we were once so excited to hug one another, our hugs just became habitual again.

For all its countless horrors, lockdown heightened my attention to the mundane, thus consecrating it into something set apart and even divine. Then the mundane's sacredness unraveled back to where it had been before: unnoticed, unholy. "The universe is full of magic things patiently waiting for our wits to grow sharper," wrote author and playwright Eden Phillpotts. Without my menagerie of usual comforts, my senses became extra sensitive to the magic of an unplanned interaction, a party I'd normally leave early, or even a grocery store run that I didn't have to meticulously choreograph in order to avoid others.

My favorite lesson of both the cardinal and of lockdown is that we all have the authority to consecrate ordinary moments. By lavishing our attention and imagination onto anything in our midst, we can transform it into something set apart.

Marilynne Robinson gave everyone permission to do this in her novel *Gilead*: "It has seemed to me sometimes as though the Lord breathes on this poor gray ember of Creation and it turns to radiance—for a moment or a year or the span of a life. And then it sinks back into itself again, and to look at it no one would know it had anything to do with fire, or light. That is what I said in the Pentecost sermon. I have reflected on that sermon, and there is some truth in it. But the Lord is more constant and far more extravagant than it seems to imply. Wherever you turn your eyes the world can shine like transfiguration. You don't have to bring a thing to it except a little willingness to see."

"Willingness to see" is what gave the cardinal its powerful name and what gives all of us the everyday ability to sanctify the mundane.

A couple of years after that muddy spring of heightened attunement to the ordinary and empty promises that we'd never take a movie theater for granted again, I learned that the world lost a very special writer, Frederick Buechner.

To be honest with you, I didn't realize he was still alive. I hadn't been keeping close tabs on him, but it turns out that he was very much living in physical form until age ninety-six when he died in his sleep at his farm in Vermont. What a way to go.

Buechner refined the art of noticing in his lifetime. He wrote about things like the wondrous creaking of a chair being tipped back on its hind legs and the miraculous compassion between strangers.

I've been wondering what has gone unnoticed since his last sleep: The optimistic hop of a bunny on a dirt trail? The last ice-cream truck of the summer lingering for an extra few minutes at dusk? The cheerful crackle and shivering ache of an Al Green record playing from an open window? A freshly mopped kitchen floor, a rusty morning sky, a muffled cry, a funeral procession, a swift soft rain?

He also wrote about things like pain. At age ten, Buechner witnessed his father's death by suicide; he also watched his daughter suffer with her own excruciating mental illness. "Whenever you find tears in your eyes, especially unexpected tears, it is well to pay the closest attention," he wrote.

He let his heart leap, and he let his heart break.

The reason I don't read the news often is because, at some point, it stopped breaking my heart. I found myself seeing world events passively, not really looking actively at the world itself. When I see/scan/consume, I fall into despair, and then anything good and beautiful feels like the exception. I feel furious, sullen, overwhelmed, numb. But not heartbroken. Breaking a heart takes time and tenderness, neither of which most media allows for.

With Buechner's death, I realized there was a big problem with how I was engaging with the world.

I resolved to start giving my full attention to the world again, the way I did during lockdown, the way the Puritans did when they stumbled onto foreign shores, the way Buechner did every day. I wanted to reclaim that strong sense of attunement and wonder, when my senses were sharp and my appreciation for the little things was overwhelming.

But once I began giving my full attention to the world, my heart broke. And having an open heart is painful, which is why I so often prefer to watch the Kardashians instead. During lockdown, I often chose to numb out and close off; I was sensitive to buying a water, noticing an ambulance, watching the news, reading a sign about another restaurant closing, being surprised by a tree's blossoming. This time, I was choosing to allow awfulness and goodness to overwhelm me.

"Here is the world. Beautiful and terrible things will happen," wrote Buechner, who surely understood that well. He was an author who looked at the world with both clear and adoring eyes. He had the ability to see his surroundings for exactly what they were—ordinary—and what they could be—set apart, holy.

My favorite writers and artists are the ones who are constantly saying "Look at this" to people around them.

They're the ones who point out everything that goes on in this world:

> Look at this courage.
> Look at this ladybug.
> Look at this exuberance.
> Look at this period in history.
> Look at this storm.
> Look at this injustice.
> Look at this porch light.

The marvel of art and literature is that both say "Look at this," but you never know if it's going to be terrible or beautiful. So many creatives are courageously present to both rather than summing up the world as a "dumpster fire" or insisting on silver linings.

Look at this, I've had to remind myself ever since regular old life resumed. I wanted to believe that I'd never take the ordinary for granted, but I quickly did, so I've had to train myself back into attention.

A morning scan of the news tells me there's a housing crisis in my city, but my heart doesn't break until I *look*. At noon, I look at a man who's asking for change outside the grocery store, and the plastic tote bag with his belongings depicts a cartoon dog in sunglasses with a speech bubble that exclaims "Ready for summer!"

My stomach tumbles down at the sight of this sweet, happy golden retriever cartoon whose joyful exclamation was not meant for this purpose. This tote bag was not meant to hold a man's belongings outside a grocery store as he asks neighbors for coins. This world was not meant to abundantly grow food that is kept in grocery stores where some can afford it and others can't.

Look at this, I tell myself, insistent on the lessons of lockdowns and the cardinals I ignored for years.

I want to allow myself to dip and even almost drown in the pain of being alive. I also want to allow myself to be awed, stunned, and overjoyed by the experience of living on earth.

Later I walk past little children crowded around a butterfly, naming its colors and gasping at its flight. There's a neighborhood cleanup at the park, where plastic is removed from ponds so that fuzzy ducklings can swim free. At the store there's a family buying new toothbrushes; I happily imagine the two large ones and two small ones in a cup by their bathroom sink. Outside, the sun illuminates the rooftop of a library.

Look at this, I tell myself.

When I let my heart participate in its full range of activities, I feel much closer to the world, much further from despair. I think about how cracks in the heart keep it from destruction the way that minor shakes in the fault lines over time prevent one colossal earthquake.

By really *looking* at what's around me with wide eyes and an open heart, I'm doing what I did so intuitively during the muddy locked-down spring.

Look at this, I tell myself. Over and over.

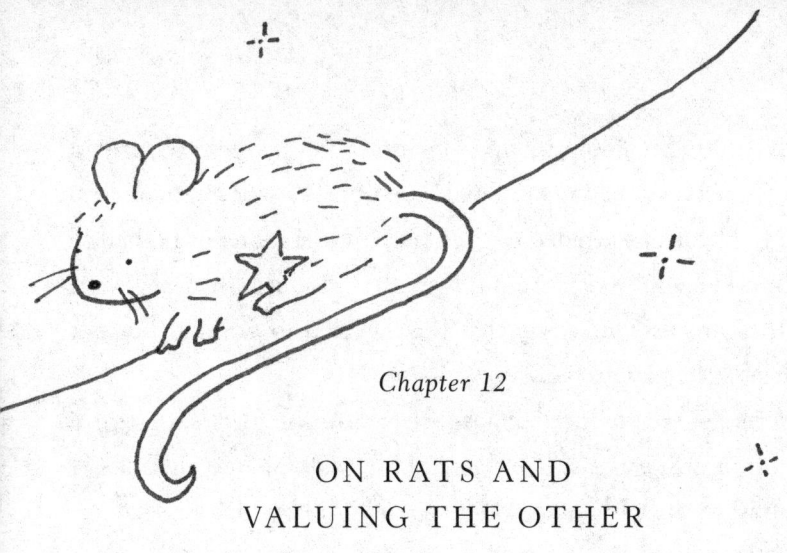

Chapter 12

ON RATS AND
VALUING THE OTHER

The day I got my wheelchair, I was elated. "Wheelchair-bound" didn't fit my experience at all; for me, it was freedom.

At the time, I was regaining strength following an autoimmune attack on my nerves, one that left me partially paralyzed and bed-bound. My legs felt impossibly heavy, like they were stuck under a boulder, and walking would be a faraway fantasy for months.

But when my occupational therapist bestowed upon me a wheelchair, the world opened up: I could go to a *café*! I could make my way to a *bus*! At the very least, I could go *outside*!

I felt like Superwoman—finally mobile, an active participant in society.

But when I actually went outside into society, I immediately noticed confusing behavior from other people. Most didn't look at me. Those who did seemed startled at first, then overcompensated with the kind of goofy, pitying look that you get when your friend wants to show you an emotional video but it's sort of embarrassing. Café patrons avoided eye contact, but the waiters who had to acknowledge my existence did so with a distance, their awkward hyperawareness indicating that they wanted to be kind but not fully associated with me.

I judged them for being so clearly uncomfortable when, a month prior, I was just like them: boldly walking into all kinds of establishments without a mobility care in the world.

Before my illness, I would either avoid or give a self-conscious, pitying grin to anyone whose mere presence startled me: a disabled person, someone living on the street, or the very elderly—people who I often looked away from.

Now I was the one who others looked away from. *But can't you see me?* I would think. *I'm normal, I'm fine, I just can't walk at the moment.* How quickly my longed-for wheelchair became an accessory that made me sort of scary.

Years later, after I had regained the use of my legs to walk, I was chatting with my hairdresser. She has a profoundly disabled daughter—a teenager who will never walk or talk and who lives at a facility far outside of New York.

"Can you believe that Lower Manhattan has only two wheelchair-accessible restaurants?" I asked. I was furious when I learned this and knew she could relate to my outrage.

My hairdresser shrugged. "Makes sense."

"Yeah, I guess," I conceded. "Space issues, high rent, a small percentage of the population, blah blah."

She shook her head. "It's because no one wants to see disabled people. It's too confronting. It's too intense. Nobody wants that reminder."

Because we were talking about her precious young daughter, my reaction was to insist otherwise, but I knew she was exactly right. I'd lived it. I knew that simply existing in a disabled body in public made people squirm—in shame, in embarrassment, in refusal to acknowledge the fact of illness and mortality and everything else that most of us desperately push away.

A distant memory surfaced. Long before my illness, I was checking into a hotel for a wedding as the peppy receptionist scanned her offerings.

"Um," she chirped, "so I have a room ready right now, but it's the accessibility room . . ."

"Okay?"

"So it would have a wider doorway, grab rails in the bathroom, that kind of thing."

"That sounds fine?" I said, not sure what was expected of me in this interaction.

"I understand if it makes you uncomfortable."

"Uh, no, I think it's okay," I said with lingering confusion.

Later I learned that another couple had declined the accessibility room. "It was so creepy," said the girlfriend as she wrinkled her nose. "Yeah, just . . . not our idea of romance," her partner chuckled.

I got it, emotionally. The rails around the toilet kind of freaked me out too, the same feeling I would get when I visited my grandpa in the nursing home and saw whiteboards in the rooms reading BLAND FOOD ONLY or BRAIN TUMOR.

But I was also curious what *exactly* about it was so "creepy" or killed the romance. Did the idea of a disability conflict with romance?

When my hairdresser casually clarified, "No one wants to see disabled people," the memory came back, as did my experience of being someone who others would rather not look at. I guess it is hard to summon romance when you're being reminded of your body's fallibility.

In the US, we shut away our seniors and severely disabled people in homes, away from the city, away from candlelit restaurants, away from romantic hotels, away from sight. Too confronting. Too intense. Easier just to keep their existence out of sight, out of mind.

And most of us would rather not try to understand our shadows. When those who we keep away manage to come into the light, beyond the invisible barricade between those in denial and those who can't afford to deny life's realities, we shudder.

I certainly have. The feeling that comes up for me when I see a person who is usually kept on the outskirts of public sight is something pretty close to disgust. It's an instantly recognizable reaction that comes from an inner murky part of myself that isn't flattering but is strongly instinctive.

If there is a universal definition of "disgust," the way there is a universal sound (a version of our guttural "ugh"), it may be: *I am not this. I am nothing like this. This is so unlike me that it will cause me to reject it.* My own physical responses to disgust are to look away, step away, and signal that *I do not belong with this.*

Susan Griffin, a feminist philosopher, recounted the experience of feeling disgust toward a person looking nauseated at a restaurant.

"I felt an anger toward her: Why was she sick in this restaurant? Why force people who are eating to participate in her mystery? I wanted to shout at her that she should go home, but of course, I did not. I was deeply ashamed of my feelings. And because of this shame I hid them away."

Recognizing the less-than-compassionate impulses that came crawling out of the shadows during this moment, Griffin acknowledged that she had projected onto the nauseated woman her own fear of death and the possibility that her body might fail too.

On my first day out to a café in my wheelchair, that's what was happening with the friend group sitting next to me, the ones who kept avoiding eye contact. My body was a reminder that bodies can fail. And that's pretty scary.

Now, years later, living in New York, I see many bodies that bring up fears of mine: people who sleep on cardboard beneath sidewalk scaffolding, people who are visibly suffering with mental afflictions that make them act erratically, people who shake from drug withdrawal, people who are old and have trouble getting across the street in time for the light to change.

That would never happen to me is a powerful belief but a flimsy lie. Who's to say we're not one accident, one injury, or one pandemic away from losing that sense of control?

In the US, 130 people a day currently die from opioid-related drug overdoses. I was prescribed an opioid for pain management when I was paralyzed. What if I had become dependent? Who can know how much it would have taken from my life?

It's natural to want to put a barrier in front of these frightening thoughts, and disgust as a response does the trick quickly. As soon as I feel the familiar agitation in my belly, I'm reminding myself, *I'm not that. That's not me.*

Disgust isn't anyone's favorite feeling, but it's an extremely useful one in human evolution. So useful, in fact, that across the languages, dialects, and accents that create the communication tying us together, the "ugh" sound unites us all. Any human from any land understands exactly how you feel about something when you emit a "yuck"-esque utterance. A look of disgust wordlessly sets a strong boundary among tribes—one of *I am not like you.* Which sounds harsh to us now, but it helped different communities communicate who belonged and who didn't.

Looks and sounds of disgust also came in handy when humans needed to signal to one another which foods were safe to eat. By gagging or even wrinkling up his nose, an early human could give his buddy a clear signal about the palatability of that leftover rhinoceros.

Now that it's safe for humans to mingle and befriend and love across different groups, and now that we have expiration dates on our food, we still use disgust to bond over rejecting "the other"—anything we strongly do not want to be associated with.

And nothing has bonded the people of New York City together quite like a single, common, "disgusting" being: rats.

Science would call our relationship with rats "commensal," meaning that one benefits the other and neither is harmed.

But ask around and you will no doubt find that people generally feel harmed by the mere existence of rats. Rat lovers are practically unheard of, and rat tolerators are considered naive. In an online forum about rat-catching, a commenter writes, "Worrying about how to kill rats ethically is of concern only to people who do not have a rat problem."

In 2023, the mayor of New York appointed a "rat czar" devoted to the rodents' eradication and invested $3.5 million in rat mitigation in Harlem alone. Crowds cheered, journalists made jokes. It seemed like it was one political issue that united rather than divided the city.

This agreed-upon social enmity toward rats is why it's considered acceptable to torture the rodents in ways that would land you a prison sentence if you did the same to a dog. Legal and socially admissible ways to "deal" with rats include glue traps, which tear off limbs as the critter dies in excruciating pain and thirst; drowning, which doesn't immediately kill the strong swimmers but instead forces them to succumb to exhaustion; and poison, which kills rats in the slow and agonizing process of internal bleeding.

This is all good and well, because rats make us feel icky.

In 2020, I got one of those miraculous pandemic deals on a Brooklyn "garden apartment" that—shockingly!—actually had a garden! As a lifelong city dweller, the prospect of tending to living things had me frantically downloading flower-identification apps (it was Helleborus) and googling how to rake leaves (I paid someone to do it).

But my first order of business was putting in several bird feeders, as my yard turned out to be a literal food court for the cardinals, jays, doves, and swallows that swarmed around my flowers.

One day, I was filling the feeders when I heard a nearby window open and saw my neighbor Bob's Santa Claus beard emerge from his living room.

"Hey, Mari!" he called. "Sorry to say this, but bird feeders are going to attract rats!"

The word made me wince. "Oh gosh, ew, thank you," I replied, as though Bob had just informed me that I'd accidentally hung an offensive flag outside my door.

Instinctively, I took down the feeder and flung it into my storage area.

Then I started questioning.

Why, exactly, did I not want to feed the rats?

If rats are dirty, aren't blue jays probably dirty too? Later I would learn that rats are less likely than humans to catch and transmit parasites and viruses. If rats were actually dangerously full of disease, most of New York would have the plague.

Was it simply that rats aren't as pretty as birds? Sure, but if you've ever studied a young brown rat zigzagging around a subway platform, you might notice that they're actually pretty cute. At least, it's conceivable that someone (me) might find them cute.

Was it that rats are dangerous? Well, they can bite, and often do when they feel threatened, but compare a few dozen recorded rat bites annually in New York to four thousand dog bites.

And if we're skeeved out by the volume of rats, why doesn't the massive population of raccoons in the city provoke the same panic?

Much of what we now know about rats' emotional and intellectual worlds is grounded in the fact that we ruthlessly experiment on them. Lab experiments use around three million rats a year as test subjects, and almost half of them cause suffering to the animals.

Strangely enough, the relentless use of rats as test subjects consistently reveals the possibility that rats have qualities previously thought to be exclusive to human beings.

For one, compassion: In a 2011 experiment, two rats were placed in separate compartments—one trapped and unable to escape, and the other free to move around. The researchers found that the free rat (the "helper") consistently freed the trapped rat, even without any reward. The helper rat even appeared distressed by its companion's discomfort.

For another: playfulness. In a fun twist on hide-and-seek, researchers at the Bernstein Center for Computational Neuroscience in Berlin taught rats to play both parts of the game. The rats had to use their memory and smarts to first *seek* out a hidden object in a maze, then switch things up and *hide* themselves to avoid getting caught. The researchers watched firsthand as rats navigated, planned, and made decisions, all for the sake of fun.

An extra-cute detail of this study is that the scientists didn't reward the rodents with food when they found the object, but rather with tickles! Throughout the game, the rats would emit little chirps of excitement, and when they received their tickle reward, they'd erupt into a fit of high-pitched rat giggles.

Even cold-hearted researchers agree that rats have distinct personalities. They express traits like shyness, boldness, mischievousness, and leadership.

An unsettling article from the Sierra Club lists just some of their talents: "laboratory experiments have shown that rats can solve complex puzzles, recognize cause-and-effect relationships, feel regret, make judgments based on perception, and understand time, space, and numbers. In online videos posted by owners of pet rats, you'll find trained rats completing agility courses, raising tiny flags by pulling tiny ropes with their delicate fingers, and 'reading' placards that instruct them either to jump onto a box or spin around. Rats even appear to engage in metacognition, meaning *rats know that they think*."

If rats have begun to remind you of another animal—one that fuels a multibillion dollar industry in the US, and that we have no problem anthropomorphizing—you may join me in wondering why Americans treat dogs like little kings and rats like trash to throw away.

"We Taiwanese are like rats," my friend's mom once said proudly. He reacted in horror. "Mom, don't say that!"

"What?" She shrugged. "We're resourceful, we adapt, we can live anywhere!" That was the first and only time I've heard a person acknowledge any similarity to a rat, despite how many qualities we share.

Lately, I've started feeling skeptical toward those who hate rats. Do people who hate rats hate something in themselves? *Who else do they hate?* I think to myself. Are rats somehow so human—too human, in fact—that people can't stand it? After all, rats scurry and burrow around us, clearly sharing an affinity for our spaces and inventiveness when it comes to what home looks like.

Or maybe on a subconscious level we know how badly we treat them and how much like us they really are. Maybe it's the same sort of confronting "yuck" feeling that I get when I see a street full of makeshift forts. I wonder why the people living there are not treated better and then why I don't treat them better.

Seeing people struggle brings up so many tough questions and feelings. *That could be me. What if it were me? Can't I just look away? Who am I if I look away? How is society treating them? How am I treating them?*

Rats may be the ultimate "other," and the questions they potentially raise are uncomfortable ones. If a society can be judged on how it treats the least within it, New York isn't looking so great.

Carl Jung's psychological concept of the "shadow" is the part of our unconscious mind that holds all the things about ourselves that we repress, whether because they are immoral, socially unacceptable, harmful, or shameful. These thoughts concealed by darkness (never to be revealed during the light of day) can overpower us until we bring them into light. For example, the adage "Admitting you have a problem is the first step" brings a person's hidden struggle out into the open so they can get help.

I wonder if rats are our shadows, the mirrors of ourselves that we can't stand and refuse to bring into the light of day. If New Yorkers started talking about rats with any feeling other than disgust, we might have to reconcile that with how we treat them—and anything or anyone else that we'd rather not see.

When I was a little girl, I loved snakes, bugs, rodents—basically anything that adults would consider distasteful, especially for a little girl. And yet, as an adult, I earnestly said "Ew!" when my neighbor told me that my bird feeder would attract rats.

What happened between childhood and now? When did I learn to hate something that once evoked affection in me? I can only imagine that somewhere, tucked between the thousands of cue cards held up as I began performing proper adulthood as a young lady, there were messages telling me I couldn't love the outcast without becoming an outcast myself.

Had I continued to love creepy-crawly things into adolescence and, God forbid, adulthood, I would have been *weird*. And we live in a society that would rather not have weird people around, even though we've learned over time that they so often have messages we all need, and desperately.

I turned my back to rats and potato bugs and lizards because, for reasons I've never known, they disgust the normal adult world.

At the same time, I also started turning away from the awkward kid in class and the strange lady on the bus. *Don't think I'm one of them,* I communicated by distancing myself.

Is this what we're all collectively doing with rats, communicating, *Don't think I'm one of them? Don't think I'm gross, ugly, dirty* or even *too natural?*

Once I started investigating my own disgust toward rats, I noticed how seamlessly my investigative questions transferred to other wobbly beliefs that kept me distant from "the other."

What was so wrong about being associated with the awkward kid in school whose brain worked differently than mine but who shared my love of lizards and elaborate make-believe scenarios? We could have played together.

Why was it important for me to scoot away from the strange lady talking to herself on the bus who adorned her body with all sorts of interesting pieces of jewelry, including several in the pile of wiry gray hair on her head? When I was a child, I would have thought she'd come straight out of a magical fairy tale. Now I admire her self-expression.

I discovered how wobbly so many of my beliefs are about the people who often hang around in subway stations. When I read about the city's "homelessness problem," I think, *Who exactly is the problem here? The ones who don't have houses, or the ones who treat unhoused humans like unwanted litter to move to the side, out of sight?*

Perhaps one day in the not-too-distant future humanity won't be so disgusted by those who don't fit in but will instead be disgusted by any attempted norm that does not love or honor the sacredness of all lives on earth.

For now, the least I can do is look directly at people in wheelchairs, the elderly, the strange bus riders, and the vulnerable folks who ask for change from a train full of subway riders desperately avoiding eye contact. I don't want anyone to believe their existence makes me uncomfortable.

And I'm sure this will strike many as very silly, but I put on a smile when I see a rat. Not because I think it knows what a smile means (although, who knows!?) but because I'm training myself to erase the invisible line I've drawn between worthy creatures and unworthy creatures, beautiful beings and ugly ones, those who delight and those who disgust me. The first, small step is a glance and a smile.

Chapter 13

ON SNOW LEOPARDS
AND ADAPTING
TO NEW PLACES

When I find myself in some sort of pickle in which I'm trying to see the situation more objectively, I often look to animals. That's because certain species mirror our human animal traits. When I research animals who share our traits, I find myself more easily understanding and even romanticizing situations rather than feeling burdened by them.

Right now I'm in desperate need of some romanticization.

You see, I have to move. Again.

A few weeks ago I learned that my new landlord is renovating this apartment and I'll have to move (a Very New York Conundrum, I've since learned).

When I got the news, I whimpered for several hours, feeling very sorry for myself and looking around to find different things to mourn: the cabinets, my bedroom window, and the cardinal who comes to that window.

This move means I will have relocated four times in the past two years, and eleven times in the past ten years. Before that, there were a dozen other moves in early adulthood, including a couple to foreign countries.

I'm getting sick of it.

Organizing all my belongings in bins and staring at blank walls while I wait for resentful friends or paid movers (who are, still, somehow resentful!) is tedious and sad at the same time. It always feels like the biggest chore that I willingly participate in.

And for what, I wonder? This time, I have no choice. But in the past, I'd choose to endure moving so . . . that I can have natural light? A roomier kitchen? An actual bathtub (but at the expense of a bathroom door that doesn't close)?

As they say, in New York there's always a trade-off. You can't get more space without sacrificing amenities; you can't have both a dishwasher *and* a washing machine; you can't get garden space without living in a glorified root cellar. I mean, some people can, but you can't.

Why do I move again, exactly?

To assess this conundrum through a more objective, generous lens, I look to snow leopards.

Snow leopards are nearly impossible to spot in the wild because they blend into their surroundings, but also because—much like me—they are never in one place for long. A snow leopard doesn't migrate, per se, but is constantly on the move around its enormous home range.

Snow leopards are solitary, so, like most humans, they make their decisions to move based on intuition and preference rather than on following the herd. They prefer to travel along ridgelines and choose their bedding sites with palatial views over the surrounding terrain (like us, snow leopards put a high value on a good view).

To be a snow leopard is to be in motion. Unlike migrating animals, they don't stop and hang out once they've reached their destination; they just keep on prowling. Like humans, they're natural explorers who self-motivate from comfort into the unknown. They want to see what's on the other side of that peak!

These "ghosts of the mountains"—so called because it is so dang hard to find them—are also adaptable. They are notoriously flexible eaters, which is a good thing considering how much their diet has had to change along with the climate. They tolerate a wide range of temperatures and could definitely give humans some pointers on how to withstand harsh seasons without becoming enraged. They have no problem with high altitudes, and they've grown some funky accessories (giant snow-shoe-esque paws and a luxuriously thick, long tail) to help them scurry around rocky terrains.

Any animal who has made it this far in evolution is a master at enduring transition. As Darwin concluded, the number-one factor of whether a species will survive is its adaptability to change.

I consider myself pretty adaptable. I get attached to new places easily and feel comfortable hopping around different cities without too much strain. But maybe I'm only so flexible because I've *had* to be?

My ambivalence toward this trait reminds me of a little monologue I read in a children's novel when I was ten. The book was called *Bloomability* by Sharon Creech. The main character Dinnie's parents send her off to school, and she has no choice but to accept it. Her resolution here stuck with me:

"I'd heard my mother tell Aunt Sandy, 'Dinnie will be fine, just fine. She's very adaptable.' As I stood there in that busy Zurich train station, I was sorry I was so adaptable, and I promised myself that I was going to stop being adaptable."

As a kid, this made me rethink my malleable personality, and when I found out I'd have to move this month, I thought about it again. Maybe I go with the flow because I don't have any other option. Maybe I never chose to be easygoing. Maybe I'd rather be a little more stubborn.

So this time I decided to try out stubbornness. I complained and fussed and, very much out of character, let my landlord know how terribly upset I was (a declaration that he was terribly uninterested in).

I showed up for my Spanish class the next day mopey and irritable, eager to share my plight with anyone who would listen, including my teacher, Andrea, who was obligated to spend the next hour with me. She very generously listened as I prattled away about the inconveniences of movers and bins and electric compa- nies and how I *just* got to know my neighbors last month.

During our next lesson, she began, "I've been thinking about your move, and I can really relate to all the irritations of moving but choosing to do it anyway. Like you, I long to be a nomad and I long for stability."

Then she shared a song called "Movimiento" by Jorge Drexler, which is a stirring piece about immigration within the continuum of human existence. He tenderly sings about how people have al- ways been on the move since the very first humans. We are an ever-moving species; it is both our nature and our tradition.

After sharing the song, Andrea said that she hoped it would give me some encouragement in the coming weeks: to remember that to be human is to be in constant motion. "Whenever you get stressed about leaving your home, maybe listen to this song," she suggested, "as something to remind you that you're not alone . . . you're joining the adventure."

In the days that followed I thought about how being a person, to be alive, really, is to be constantly shifting—with seasons, with work, with health, with relationships, with the dream of sunshine or proximity to water.

Those of us who can't sit still may feel like there's something wrong with us, but restlessness is how our world erupted in varied languages and cultures and dreams.

Like snow leopards, humans are drifting, traveling, ever-changing creatures who often struggle to master permanency. For some of us, we stop living when we stop moving. Humans evolved impec- cably to adapt.

Yet as much as humans are wired for impermanence, like snow leopards, we're also highly observant and highly sensitive to the small things that fill our days and hearts. I'm not sure if snow leopards fondly reflect upon the mountain where they roamed last summer. All I know for sure is that it causes me pain to move, and yet I keep doing it anyway. And this one is especially tough.

I moved to this garden unit in a Brooklyn brownstone last year and filled the stagnant winter days with burrowing into my new home.

Adorning a living space is one of my treasured methods of self-expression, but it also serves a greater purpose: creating a home is self-parenting. I make a home for myself that is as joyful and safe as I can, a refuge for the insecurities of both inner child and adult.

In particular, I designed my current apartment to be a sanctuary of healing and comfort. While making decisions about where to put furniture and decor, I would step outside my door and reenter as many times as it took to figure out what felt intuitive to me as I came into the space. Did I want to sit down here or there? Where did my eyes want to go? In short, I decorated how I wanted to feel.

Now, as I force bulging boxes closed with shreds of packing tape and meagerly protect my tchotchkes with layers of newspaper, I think about the moments that happened at this home: taking off my coat when I got in and seeing Sunny's cheerful ears perk up from behind her curled body; spreading too much butter on seedy bread in the morning while I listened to the gurgle of my coffee maker and a familiar podcast at the same time; returning to my soft, safe bed after a day pierced with shame; scribbling a thank-you note to my neighbors who left out a plate of cookies in the foyer; hearing a friend's voice through my phone and laughing as I pressed my back against the protective base of a velvet armchair; witnessing dishes accumulate in a tower in the sink as houseguests enthusiastically gobbled up the food that I made earlier that day.

I also consider my own species, how we wander around land with the range of a snow leopard, and yet we have much stronger sentimental attachments to where we've come from. A textbook chart shows that Homo sapiens made their way from central Africa to West Asia, then up to the Arctic Circle. Another group broke off and joined those Indigenous to South Asia in Australia. While these big moves happened over centuries, without the help of a moving truck, they still must have involved so much grief. To be a human is to say goodbye a lot of times. And our ancestors had to say goodbye constantly.

In the grand scheme of things, my move is minor. I can always go back to my old neighborhood and say hi to the folks at the pet supply store; I can even stay in touch with the neighbors who used to bring me cookies. But as natural, common, and now easy (relative to the grueling undertaking it was in the past) as it is to move, I'm very sad. I'm sad because of what I'm losing: the glistening four-thirty p.m. autumnal light, the stove that worked really well, the door that didn't work at all, and the resilient chirp of 130-year-old floors.

I need to say goodbye.

A few years ago, I received a wedding invitation in the mail that was addressed to someone else; I assumed it was for the tenant who lived in my apartment before me, and I did some sleuthing to find her so I could send it her way. When we finally connected, she messaged me how much she loved the home she'd left: "I had the best nights of my life there, learned to cook there, fell in love there, became myself there. I hope it's as magical for you as it was for me."

I told her that I knew someone wonderful must have lived there before because I could feel the walls' lovely energy. I've found that even people who don't believe in things like a wall's lovely energy admit that they can tell when a home has been well loved.

For that reason, I do rituals when moving in and out. I have tremendous respect for the space I enter as a new home, trusting it to protect me. And when I leave, I literally thank the home and ask it to protect the next person.

So with gratitude, I pass through this space as others did before me. I ask the apartment to protect the next person. Maybe someday, someone will wonder if anyone had the best nights of her life here, learned to cook here, fell in love here, became herself here.

(Future tenant: It was me.)

Chapter 14

ON DONKEYS
AND QUESTIONING
INTELLIGENCE

The waiter at Rústica was sick of me.

I'd watched him joyfully greet others into the open-air vegetarian café with a roble tree twisting through the middle of its three stories. He stretched out his arms Jesus-style to embrace the regulars with a big back-patting hug and kiss on the cheek.

The first couple of times I sat on the top floor with the top of the tree brushing my table, I thought for sure he seemed mildly intrigued by me. I imagined a whole monologue going through his head: *What is this gringa doing in this part of Mexico? Where is she staying? What is she doing?*

Just as I wondered how he'd found his sense of style: striped linen pants paired with various band T-shirts, a handlebar mustache, and an attempt at dreadlocks—or maybe a matted ponytail that rarely came undone. He sang in fake falsetto as he cleaned tables and put on a British accent when he ushered in visitors, "Welcome!"

But the number of times I blundered—or, rather, bludgeoned—my attempts to converse with him in Spanish seemed to have turned me into a pesky chore rather than an intriguing guest worthy of his dramatics. He looked impatient when I ordered, and when he waved goodbye it was more like a shooing away.

Little did he know the sea of language I was thrashing around in under the surface of my stutters and hand gestures. Inside my mind, I recited Spanish poetry to myself, practiced complex sentences, even had imaginary conversations with the waiter about his past troubadouring life.

But on the outside, either I was mute with insecurity or my words sloshed out from my mouth as though I'd poured them out too quickly. Then I would bite my lip and return to my green smoothie, trying not to bother anyone else with my failures.

This was as close as I've felt to being too much work to understand. Well, at least in a literal way. I usually feel like too much work for most people, but not because I have trouble articulating myself. Articulating my feelings precisely and elaborately is exactly what makes me quite laborious for those around me to talk to, I'm sure.

But in the saga between me and the waiter, the grief I caused him was on a more basic level: He had little patience for my flailing around with his beautiful language. It took effort for him to piece what I was saying into sense, and he would rather not have to. I didn't blame him. But it left me silent and discouraged.

There are millions of people who feel this way all the time, people who hold oceans in their minds that leak out when prompted or demanded but otherwise stay behind the levee of minimal speech and a seemingly blank expression.

I used to teach gymnastics to a group of older children, maybe eight to ten, that magical age when personality begins shining through in hyperbole and limit testing. But while the other kids' faces often resembled exaggerated masks with clown-size smiles or outrageous pouts of disappointment, Eleanor's remained quiet and bare. While her classmates squealed and sang or displayed goody-two-shoes people-pleasing, Eleanor just sat, silent.

Her parents thought maybe someday she'd feel compelled to join in, but she never did. We instructors were all encouraged to invite Eleanor into the activity, but we approached that suggestion as a lost cause to begin with; she wouldn't even nod yes or no, only continue to stare ahead from her chair against the wall.

Kids and adults alike quickly gave up on talking to her. She was tough on our egos; it felt vulnerable to set ourselves up to be ignored and frustrating to get nowhere after a few attempts. She'd sit there, unfazed, while us adult teachers would get our feelings hurt by an eight-year-old who couldn't make us feel instantly good about ourselves.

I suspected Eleanor must have so much feeling and perceptiveness inside; she was a watcher and listener. But I didn't know how to enter her world.

One afternoon her parents brought along her twin brother, Max, when they picked her up from gymnastics. As soon as I opened the door to release the children, hyped up and screaming from an afternoon of literally crawling all over one another, Eleanor got up and lightly trotted over to Max. He embraced her and she smiled. She made a couple of soft grunting sounds and Max turned to his parents. "She's thirsty," he announced.

I hope I didn't blurt "What?" out loud, because that's what crashed into my head: confusion, revelation, witness to the miraculous.

Over the next few minutes, while Eleanor's parents took care of a bill, Max responded to Eleanor's hums and subtle facial expressions with clear responses. When he started singing "Happy Birthday" to her, I asked, "Oh my gosh, is it your birthday, Eleanor?"

Max responded matter-of-factly. "No, it's just her favorite song and she wanted me to sing."

"How could you tell she wanted you to sing, Max?"

He looked at me skeptically. "I just . . ." he started, then shrugged.

It was so obvious to him, her closest friend for a lifetime and from before birth. He'd spent most of his living hours by her side; of course he would understand her wants and preferences, and most likely her fears and pains. But without language, and without facial expressions that could be connected to any of the cartoon emotions on the HOW ARE YOU FEELING TODAY? poster, I was mystified by the key he held to her world.

Or maybe it wasn't a key at all, maybe there was no door. Maybe it was something more akin to a birdsong, a dance, a set of paints with colors I didn't know existed.

In a different family at a different time, where would the world have placed Eleanor? In an institution, far away from sight, to play blocks all day as her only stimulation?

Not long ago, even highly verbal autistic individuals were cast aside, seemingly unable to emote as much as the rest of us and therefore considered more primal or animal-like than full human participants in society.

But now we know that people on the autism spectrum often feel so strongly that they end up shutting down because they are overwhelmed by stimulation, and by their own empathy. A person picking up on so many subtleties, patterns, and stimuli might withdraw due to sensory overload, and other people may then wrongly assume that the person doesn't want to socialize.

Human brains are lazy. We like our assumptions to be met, our expectations to be fulfilled, and patterns to be followed to make life easier so that we can autopilot our way through interactions. We also crave being easily understood; it makes us feel good. So when we encounter someone who expresses themselves in a different way—in a language that hasn't found us yet—it can irritate, even threaten, us.

Even nonautistic people are asked, "Why are you being quiet?" When we're busy yapping about our day or our mouths are full of croutons, our dinner date's silence not only threatens our pride but also unnerves us and can creep us out; we don't attempt to appreciate what's not being said and we don't explore the intricacy of nonverbal communication.

Some animals sing, some rattle, some coo, and some, like us, cry and imitate and yawn. It takes time to learn all the sounds and punctuations of silence the universe chants, and we never will if we don't tune our ears to what we don't understand.

I first heard a donkey bray at a sanctuary under the rolling blue hills of Connecticut, where six donkeys were living, having been rescued after being raised in Pennsylvania, auctioned off in Mexico, then boarded on a ship to Korea for their hides to be used in an antiaging gel. Once so scrawny that the sanctuary couldn't even tell that one of them was pregnant, they now scampered with pudgy bellies on full display up to their caretaker, Julie, who invited me to help feed them lunch.

As they brayed in a choral round, flashing large, funny teeth and lifting their heads like gospel singers in praise, they actually sounded exactly like *Hee-haw, hee-haw.*

"Best sound in the world," Julie said with a smile, and it was then I realized that the loud braying meant "happiness." I might have mistaken this wild wail for agony or crippling hunger, but the way they mobbed her with head bops, not debilitating to the ones my cat gives my legs when I get home, confirmed an elated reunion with their human pal.

Historically, donkeys are employees. Like other "beasts of burden," they've been domesticated to labor for humans: pulling things, carrying us, moving goods up and down hills, posing for selfies in Santorini and Sicily. Donkeys are thought to easily carry half their weight, so they are loaded up with cases of soda and boxes of oranges to wind through cobbled streets all around the Mediterranean and Middle East.

In many parts of the world, donkeys squarely belong in the "useful" category of the useful/not useful binary that humans have divided the natural world into. We value any flora or fauna that we have a need for and generally ignore the rest, as though the world were created to orient entirely to our needs. Once the living thing is needed no longer, we deal with it in a variety of ways: trucking baby donkeys to hide auctions in Mexico, kicking pigeons around the sidewalk, keeping working shepherd dogs inside Manhattan studios, and dumping mouse-chasing barn cats on the side of the road when the farm sells.

In North America, where we once imported donkeys and pigeons from Europe to use as our mail carriers and plantation plows, we now look at both as the animal equivalent of fax machines. Nostalgic at best, useless at worst.

And while the pigeon may be excused for being a bit of a scatterbrain, the donkey has the absolute gall to be stubborn, hard to train, and resistant to any activity removed from its natural behavior (those activities include being ridden, carrying heavy objects, holding up its feet for horseshoe care, traveling in a trailer, or being led into unknown territory).

After I enjoyed watching the sanctuary donkeys munching on the trash bin of hay that their caretaker and I poured into their trough,

Julie asked if I wanted to take a couple donkeys on a walk along the riverside trail.

Twist my arm!

I had high hopes of bonding with one of these beautiful creatures and maybe even eliciting the same head bop that Julie received from all six of them at once, so I was thrilled to put a leash on the middle-aged mare, Daisy, who seemed far more interested in joining the other donkeys as they attempted to yank carrot shreds out from their treat-filled puzzle toy.

Daisy was still fuzzy with a winter coat, a cozy layer of thick brown tufts growing loyally to the cross shape on her back, the same shared by every donkey since birth. She pulled a little on her leash, startling me with her strength, but Julie just laughed it off as she coaxed Daisy's son, Little Blue, onto the trail ahead of us.

The donkeys walk this trail at least five times a week for exercise. It's the only route they've ever known in their lives; they'd lived in pens until their arrival at the sanctuary.

Yet still, every time so much as a twig presented itself in the trail, Daisy would abruptly stop. She might vocalize something like a soft soprano bray for Little Blue, and then purposefully walk far around it even if I pulled her leash back to the middle.

"So there's something you should know about donkeys," called out Julie, who walked assertively in her red plaid shirt, faded Levi's, and cowboy boots. "They don't care what you think."

She paused on the trail to elaborate. "When you're riding a horse, you can command her to jump off a cliff and she'll do that. You can lead her anywhere, make her leap, go faster, put her at risk. You're her boss; we bred fear out of her. But donkeys won't trust *you* to keep them out of trouble. They are super cautious. Doesn't matter that they've been on this path a million times. They are looking for danger."

Awww, I thought, *anxious little thing*, and stroked Daisy's neck with the back of my palm.

I suppose that's why they are called stubborn; they aren't interested in your commands if they aren't feeling it themselves. You can lead a horse to water but you can't make it drink, whereas you can't even lead a donkey to water if it senses any risk.

People generally think of donkeys as troublesome because of their stoicism—their disinterest in showing and communicating their emotional state.

Their changes in behavior are subtle, and maybe counterintuitive. For instance, a slight widening of their eyes might be misread as curiosity when it may actually mean stress or fear. A lack of movement away from an unknown object might be misread as confidence rather than a reduced flight response.

Compared to horses, donkeys show a limited response to pain, illness, and fear, and may even appear catatonic when in distress. When threatened, donkeys plant their feet firmly on the ground while they assess the situation at hand. What looks like stubbornness to us is likely an expression of fear.

Julie knew all this, but she also knew the subtleties of each donkey's emotional range. While Little Blue looked completely content to me, she sighed and confidently called back, "He's getting tired and grumpy." I didn't even ask how she knew. I guessed it was hard to explain, like Eleanor's brother Max shrugging at my logistical question about his communication system with his non-verbal sister.

The topic of animal feelings has been long debated. Science has a hard time scrounging up evidence for something that probably can't be proven. For the sake of how humans treat animals, it would be nice to imagine that their emotions are not nearly as developed as ours, and that the pain they feel is on a much smaller scale. Then we could experiment on them in peace, and carelessly eat meat from factory slaughterhouses.

But all intuitive signs point to that not being the case. Peter Wohlleben, author of *The Inner Life of Animals*, concludes, "And so, as I see it, there is only one kind of grief, pain, or love. . . . 'Aha,' the scientist might interject at this point, 'but we have no proof.' That's true, but there will never be any proof. I can't even prove that you feel the same way as I do."

As a product of a society that values logic over intuition, I once would have countered: "Otters protect their babies out of maternal instinct, not love." But I'm learning that scientific research into animal emotions and intelligence has barely scratched the surface of the *type* of feeling and intellect animals possess. Could it be that they actually know and feel far more than we do, in a different set of shades that our eyes cannot even perceive?

After all, as Jonathan Balcombe writes in *Second Nature*, "Humbling as it may be, for all our vaunted brain power, humans emerge as nothing special in the sensory sweepstakes. Our senses of vision, hearing, smell, taste, and touch are middling, at best."

I've often heard the intelligence of a pig compared to that of a three-year-old human child. But when I asked about this at the Catskill Animal Sanctuary in upstate New York, the tour guide paused.

Sweetly and diplomatically, the guide with worn Wellington boots and a purple bob answered, "That could be true, but I don't like to compare animal intelligence that way . . . it doesn't really make sense, right? Because animals just do completely different things from humans. Like, okay, so pigs can smell eleven feet underground. They can even communicate through the ground to others far away. Can you really compare that to the abilities of humans? Animals are intelligent in the ways they need to be. Pigs don't need to learn spelling, although I'm sure someone has tried to teach them. They're intelligent for the things that matter to them, just like us."

I softened, and instantly regretted every pork chop I'd ever eaten. I remembered a documentary called *The Truffle Hunters* about pigs who can locate and extract truffle mushrooms in the forest, much to the appreciation of fancy chefs all over Europe. They can smell the fungi growing feet underground and know how to unearth the valuable fruit. Imagine if a human could do this: they would at least make the six o'clock news with their weird, specific superhuman talent.

I would later read the work of Frans de Waal, who studied animal intelligence and morals. He wrote that we make judgments on the smartness of animals based on how well they do at human tasks, like counting numbers or speaking French. He argued that the human-superiority method is outdated and instead made a convincing case for assessing each species' intelligence on its own terms.

He posited that if you asked a squirrel to design an intelligence test, they would say, "Okay, well hide as many things as you can. And then we'll give you three months off and see if you can remember the locations of them." Because that's what squirrels do with their intelligence: they hide thousands of nuts all over the park and find them again a few months later. And that's a very complicated, cognitively complex thing to do. (Can you go a *week* without losing your keys?!)

If humans took the squirrel test, we'd definitely come out on the bottom. We're the ones who define intelligence, and define ourselves as the smartest species, but there's not much evidence that we are.

We don't have the biggest brains, we're not the only species with self-awareness (even manta rays will flap around to see what they look like at different angles in a mirror), and we apparently haven't figured out how to live in symbiotic relationship with other animals.

Humans aren't even the most emotional creatures. Orcas have an emotional-processing center, and that part of their brain is much larger than it is in humans, and it's overdeveloped proportionally as well. So there are other animals who could be having much more intense or more complicated emotions or greater emotional ranges, maybe even feeling emotions that we humans don't have access to.

We tend to put a higher value on animals who we call "smart," but only smart in a ridiculously limited definition. Any intelligence that doesn't serve our needs directly doesn't seem to command our respect.

When we're children, we gravitate toward animals. We carry around stuffed animals like our life depends on it, and we reach out to pat stray kitties on the back even if our parents warn us about germs.

But when we sever ourselves from the rest of animals, we start regarding animals as resources. We reject our wild-animal-ness and rank our own skills far above those of any creatures, even the creatures whose skills clearly exceed ours and who fit into their environment with greater ease. While our intellectual evolution has tried to reshape the world to fit us, true evolution would have us fit back into the world as it is.

Daisy never gives me a head bop. I don't think she's been trying to bond with me as much as I have with her. I speak gently to her—"Good girl, I know that stick is so scary"—and I stroke her shoulder as we walk. Maybe she's enjoying my company a great deal or maybe she's still dreaming of those carrot shreds in the puzzle. I don't know.

But after I take off her leash and she moves her head around and rolls her lips, I don't assume I'm projecting when I whisper my reply: "I had a good time too."

Stoic as they may seem, donkeys aren't as mysterious as we

think they are. They get frustrated when they don't feel like working, and they feel good when we rub them or give them treats. They get thirsty after laboring in the sun, and they're happy to see someone they know and love.

But then wouldn't you seem stoic too in the company of someone who never tried to understand your communication, refused to learn your particularities, and didn't recognize your pain because they didn't express it in the exact same way?

I remember practically tugging on Eleanor to say something, to do something, to let me know what she thought and felt and if I was doing a good job. But she didn't care about affirming me; she cared about speaking through the only person who was patient enough to put his ear against a shell to hear the ocean inside her.

I think about all the people I've met who are socially liberated to say, "I hate cats," and why? Because cats threaten the ego by not doing exactly what we want, when we want, in the manner in which we want?

I, like anyone, have gotten frustrated when people don't smile, and cats don't come up to my lap, and donkeys don't bray with delight when I approach their pen, and a little nonverbal girl doesn't trust me enough to join in a group setting that has never proven itself to be safe for her.

But the rewards of spending time with a being who doesn't immediately cater to my pride are endless—in fact, the joy of my life. The time I've spent with patients in the hospital who communicate only with their eyes, with my pet cat whose cues will take many more years to learn, my friend's daughter who acts what she's feeling rather than says it, and donkeys who haven't been domesticated long enough to make perfect sense to humans—this is time I've treasured the most. I've gotten to access inner worlds, however briefly, and for that I am so grateful.

Learning to speak the language of subtlety, which might actually be a language of color, or a language of coos and grunts, or a language of glances and heartbeats, has brought me even more deeply into my own world. It's a world where I remember the ocean inside each of us, and where a blank stare doesn't have to threaten me but instead can beckon me into the wonder of silence and divine mystery of another.

Chapter 15

ON PIGEONS
AND BRINGING
THE OUTSIDERS IN

"The Pigeon Man" is a New York City fixture. He's not one specific person, but rather a character who manifests in various individuals around the city's parks. While certain park patrons may claim they know the *original* Pigeon Man, their argument is as useless as a declaration of the best pizza slice in the city, or the most authentic bodega. Everyone has a different answer.

The Pigeon Man I've seen most often covers himself daily with bird feed on a bench in the middle of a Manhattan park that locals mostly use as a commute shortcut. As others shuffle through, the man sits surrounded by pigeons, and he looks blissed-out among their pecking and squawking around his head—something the rest of us would consider a Hitchcockian nightmare. Passersby either avoid him completely or stop to stare; he's an oddity, and his affinity for these unloved urban birds fascinates mischievous children and buttoned-up businesspeople alike.

I imagine he feels camaraderie with them—a filthy city bird himself. He too eats junk food and scraps and finds his way into train stations and subways so he can keep warm. He's beautiful like them, colorful and iridescent with his purple locs and fluorescent backpack.

As someone who feels more comfortable on the edges than in the center, my heart goes out to this man and his bird community who have both been pushed farther and farther from the center to the point where many of us might literally not even see them.

While the richest of the rich used to keep pigeons in cages as a sign of wealth (they were rare and exclusive), now most people associate this colorful dove with the poor.

In *Mary Poppins*, it's a weird old woman who invites people to join her in feeding the birds, tuppence a bag. All the well-to-do Londoners scurry past her to dodge being asked for birdseed money; it's only the children who stop and feel moved to feed these city pests.

In various parks around New York City, a friend to pigeons is someone who the rest of us may think of as "not mentally there" enough to hold a job. It's no surprise that they find companionship with an intelligent, compassionate, physically beautiful species who has been cast aside as useless and a nuisance.

Humans domesticated pigeons thousands of years ago. People took them into their homes—the wealthiest homes, at that—in Europe, Asia, and North Africa. They used pigeons to carry messages, and worldwide respect for them peaked during the world wars. In World War I, a group of US soldiers were lost behind enemy lines in France and found themselves barraged by friendly fire. They sent a pigeon called Cher Ami to provide coordinates and call off the attack. Cher Ami was shot down, blinded in one eye and with serious injuries to his leg and chest, but still managed to take flight again and get to their allies with the message of their location, which led to almost two hundred lives being saved. In World War II, a pigeon named Winkie saved an entire crew that had crash-landed at sea, earning her the PDSA Dickin Medal.

But after the world wars, communication tech rapidly evolved past sending birds into the air. When humans' use for pigeons became zero, the fully domesticated birds joined the wild pigeon populations in cities.

They adapted impressively well, changing their nesting grounds to buildings, switching their diet to scrap food, and dealing with pollution.

While human city dwellers like a bit of nature here and there, they also like to control it. And it's pretty hard to control a massive human-made bird population. In the sixties, public perception of pigeons totally plummeted, and it became socially acceptable to kick pigeons and drench them in chemicals.

People bred pigeons specifically so they would hang around us. Now we get annoyed—even outraged—that they still do. They are the VCRs, the heavy black-and-white TVs, the CD-ROM drives of animals. Once essential, they now take up space in our homes. If they would just leave our parks and moldings, we could modernize in peace.

Unlike rats, most people generally (and resentfully) tolerate the existence of pigeons, but very few people love or care about street pigeons. That is, seemingly except for people who are on the fringes of society. Those who cultivate relationships with wild city pigeons are most likely to be already disconnected from their surrounding community due to mental illness or poverty, so why not show favor to another outcast? Maybe they feel more empathy toward a creature who's considered worthless because it isn't "useful."

When I think about the "usefulness" of a species, I recall well-meaning arguments for looser immigration policies in the US.

ALBERT EINSTEIN WAS AN IMMIGRANT, I've seen on posters and in political propaganda. Surely there are brilliant minds and once-in-a-generation artists and future tech billionaires among the new Americans who line up at immigration offices, and there are also full-time mothers and trash collectors and kids who can't contribute to the workforce yet.

There are disabled seniors who have incredible singing voices but can't do physical labor, and there are twentysomethings who are writing prodigies and speak multiple languages but haven't yet mastered English.

If we demand productivity even from the weary humans entering our country, surely we have little tolerance for the "useless" animals crowding our cities.

Pigeons are not quite as humanlike as rats (or dogs), but they

are bred even better than butter-yellow Labrador puppies to accompany us. They love us because we've trained them to. They're
in our spaces because we wanted them to be.

Now that their résumés are outdated, most people would love
to send them to a pigeon nursing home where they could be out of
sight, mind, and moral reflection. But in our plazas they stay, useful only as reminders of our failure to care for the animals we bred
to care for us.

Perhaps the problem with those "rats with wings" (and the
ones without!) lies with us, not them.

I used to visit a group home in DC dedicated to providing soulful
care for adults with intellectual disabilities.

Some volunteers mistook them for angels; I knew better. They
were flawed people, not because of their disabilities but for the
humanness that we all share: their occasional greediness, stubbornness, interruptions. I knew better than to call them "pure,"
"innocent," or "childlike," but I did see something in them that
nondisabled people lacked.

Many of them were hyperperceptive, with memories that would
rival a history book. A few of them had exceptional senses, able to
smell the hidden chocolate in a cupboard above reach. One eighty-
four-year-old could recall the names of everyone he'd ever met. I'm
not kidding; we would page through his childhood yearbook, and
without looking at the credits, he'd list every first name for every
photo.

How we decide what or who is valuable to us in society has almost everything to do with how "useful" they are. It's as though the worthiness of human life itself isn't quite enough . . . they also have to contribute on a level that we have decided is meaningful to us at this moment in time.

In society it's not particularly *useful* that Don could remember your name, or that Elva could identify each spring flower by closing her eyes and smelling it, or that Victor enjoyed the feeling of shuffling cards and did so long after any game was over. But their worlds are not our world, and my world is not your world, and no sentient being should have to prove how useful they are in order for us to treat them gently.

Reflect on what you consider useful and not, then think about how you treat both. What in nature is useful or not? Which animals are useful or not? Which people are useful or not? Radical prophets throughout history, like Jesus, were constantly questioning our perspective on what mattered and what didn't, who was "clean" and who wasn't, who belonged and who didn't. And, let's face it, prophets in their time have never exactly been considered totally normal and socially acceptable.

Someday I'm not going to be useful. You're not either. Even with impeccable health and a job that shines in a capitalistic framework, everyone gets old. Everyone gets sick. Everyone wonders how others—even their loved ones—will treat them when they can't provide what they used to.

People used to prize pigeons so highly that the most hoity-toity elite would proudly display their pets in windows of living rooms as a status symbol. Then, when pigeons became a bit more working class, they received the same public praise and even medals that firefighters, teachers, and soldiers are awarded for a generous job well done.

Now most buildings have spikes so pigeons can't land. Very few people feed them, so they eat literal garbage that is terrible for their little bodies. When they hover over sidewalk grates for warmth, people stomp them away—or worse. Every day in New York, I see pigeons with drooping wings; broken beaks; damaged feet; in winter, frostbite; in summer, dehydration; in all seasons, suffering.

And, every day in New York, when I walk out of my apartment, I see my own neighborhood's version of The Pigeon Man. He's a night janitor at a nearby condo who gets off his shift around eight a.m. For an hour or two, he sits on a bench in Brooklyn Bridge Park as the sun rises, and he distributes at least half his breakfast to the local pigeons.

He alone is a striking sight. He has covered his entire body in thick, labyrinthine tattoos, including all over his face and the bald top of his head. He has facial piercings I didn't know were possible, like on his forehead and temples and under his eyes, and he hooks horns and plastic spirals through those piercings. He is tall and large and always wears a bright orange vest. Not one thing about his physical presence is unremarkable.

Honestly, when I first saw him, he scared me. I bet he scares a lot of people. So I go out of my way to say hi to him—as a signal to myself and others that nobody's physical appearance should be scary. And once I started seeing his pigeon routine, I knew my fear was hilariously misdirected to begin with. He coos at them, beckons them, and shares his meal with them.

I think of him every time I see people shoo away stray cats, try to stomp on rats, set out glue traps, or purposefully smash pigeon nests to the ground. All of that exists as an external illustration of what my culture says is useful or not.

But this Pigeon Man—all the Pigeon People—also exist, and they illustrate what a culture of care and compassion *could* look like: looking out for all beings, no matter what they provide.

Chapter 16

ON WOLVES
AND BECOMING
NATURAL

I'm a dog person."

I've heard that phrase often since the very first time I invited a friend over to my house and they looked puzzled—if not outright alarmed—at the cat in my room.

Oh yeah, I reasoned, *there are dog people and there are cat people. That makes sense.*

Then as I grew older, it started making less sense. Not only are they completely different animals, but I started noticing that self-proclaimed "dog people" wouldn't even bother trying to interact with a cat. I started feeling self-conscious about my feline proclivities with the discovery of the phrase "crazy cat lady" and the baffling stereotype that people with cats are pathetic and desperate.

But then I learned a fact that changed my entire relationship to all pets: Dogs have been domesticated for 130,000 years. Cats have been domesticated for ten thousand years. Besides donkeys, cats might be the very last domesticated animals, and like donkeys, they have the reputation for being stubborn, annoying, and very selective.

Can we blame them? In the grand scheme of earth, ten thousand years is the length of a TikTok video compared to the entire series of your grandparents' home movies. Cats and donkeys are still just beginning to figure out if humans are occasionally trustworthy, much less how to impress us with tricks and clear-to-us facial expressions.

When it comes to domestication and human relationships, no animal can compete with dogs, who humans meticulously engineered to meet our physical and emotional needs to the point of their own detriment.

Thousands of years ago, our ancestors had a good thing going with wolves.

We weren't even the ones to say hello first. You can probably imagine that ancient humans spent a great deal of their lives avoiding anything that had fur and sharp teeth, and they weren't exactly tossing Frisbees in wolves' directions, hoping for a fireside cuddle.

Rather, wolves started loitering around human settlements in Germany and Siberia when they caught on that these human creatures threw out their leftovers, an all-too-easy way to grab a snack.

Scientists believe that over time, people warmed to wolves through their playful pups. Untrained wolf puppies retrieve a ball based on human cues (what scientists call "human-directed behavior"), mimicking how early humans figured out that wolves could be pals. This is why play has always been central to our relationships with dogs. (The same could not be said for the saber-tooth tigers who also roamed around Siberia.)

The tale of how dogs evolved from wolves could be titled "Survival of the Friendliest." Our ancestors had no hesitation in hiding from the aggressive canines, but they formed meaningful bonds with the sweeter ones. In just a few generations, the descendants of the sweet ones began taking on their own characteristics: floppy ears, wagging tails, and the remarkable ability to read us.

Wolves seemed happy to self-domesticate, inviting themselves over to the human pack and volunteering to keep out dangerous animals, all while preserving their own kind. Humans were delighted to have extra help with hunting, and the bond was easy. We really could have stopped there and called it a day.

Thousands of years later, an influencer carries her toy Pomeranian in a purse down the street. A newlywed couple keeps an Australian shepherd—built for daylong sprinting—in an apartment. A child pleads to his parents to buy a golden retriever puppy from a breeder, while hundreds of shelter dogs are euthanized in the next suburb over.

Humans had the once-in-a-centimillennium gift of a helpful companion creature who was not only lifesaving but also fun and cute! And, through aggressive selective breeding, we turned the tamed wolf into hundreds of varieties of dogs—many of whom suffer terrible physical problems because of inbreeding.

We humans like to believe that dogs are similar to us, maybe even the most similar species. It's a really flattering idea! Dogs are as social and playful as we are, but they are also naturally loyal, selfless, protective, funny, unconditionally loving, and far more visually pleasing than a boa constrictor or an elephant seal.

In reality, we are far more similar to rats than to dogs. Whereas the world's most hated rodent thrives in cities, will give their life for another of their kind, and loves the same shelter and diet that humans enjoy, dogs need specialized care and will only sacrifice their lives for their owners because we've bred them to. They seem to "smile" because, through selective breeding, dog enthusiasts have created them to look happy. If dogs look emotional, in the way that people understand outward emotion, it's by design.

Our extensive manufacturing of a dog to be cuter, smaller, more golden, or less autonomous reflects our most egotistical impulses. We want nature to look like us, cater to us, become us.

Dog breeding has caused all kinds of health problems in our supposed best friends, ranging from Boston terriers, whose puppy-like round heads cause serious seizures, to French bulldogs that literally cannot give birth naturally because we like the way they have big heads and small pelvises.

And why? Weren't domesticated wolves enough?

If I can summon the most compassionate read of this dog situation, maybe it's that existing in nature was tough for humans for a really long time. It's tough for everyone out there, but people also had to create culture and figure out religions and think of stories to explain why they were in Siberia in the first place and what math is. All this while experimenting with poisonous versus non-poisonous berries and running away from gigantic animals who actively wanted to eat them.

So here's this wolf, and people are doing a fantastic job at making him just a little more palatable here and there. I imagine it's hard to stop manipulating nature once you get going, after you see what evolution can do naturally. Why not take it into your own hands? Why not create a wolf with a prettier color, with a more smushed face, with a softer bark?

Take the brow example. Ed Yong writes, "Dogs have a facial muscle that can raise their inner eyebrows, giving them a soulful, plaintive expression. This muscle doesn't exist in wolves. It's the result of centuries of domestication, in which dog faces were inadvertently reshaped to look a bit more like ours. Those faces are now easier to read, and better at triggering a nurturing response."

That seems innocent enough. I mean humans have done weirder things with their powers than make dogs look pathetic so we remember to feed them. But we can't pretend for a moment that modern dog breeds are not the result of elaborate experiments with our own selfish interests in mind, at the expense of the dog's health and comfort.

And we certainly can't pretend that they are similar to us. Rather, they are products of our egos and mirrors of our greed.

"We don't deserve dogs," humans say. But we *constructed* dogs.

Some families of wolves evolved beautifully to accompany early humans but still retained their wildness and their wolf-ness. Once humans began selectively breeding wolves to become specific types of dogs, the animals lost any sense of wildness and wolf-ness. Now they're probably almost as human as they are critter, whereas cats still have most of their critter-ness. Is there any wonder why dogs, designed to please humans, are more popular?

You may have guessed by now that this topic really grinds my gears. But the root of my grumpiness is sadness. Because we created dogs to be so affectionate, I want every dog to be in a loving home. I get bummed out when people continue to prioritize aesthetics or trends in animals over a real need, to shelter and feed and love the millions that have been discarded for failing to hit an arbitrary ideal that we invented.

Yet dogs still love us. Even if we have mass-produced them to do so, they continually demonstrate love, and in the exact way that we happen to understand it. (Cat owners, here's your moment to feel superior that you care for a being who hasn't been designed to pander to you.)

For all we've done to plunder it, nature has never given up on us. Dogs still act like they've won the lottery on their birthday when their person comes home from work, even if, because of people, some of them can't breathe comfortably through their noses. Now that's unconditional love.

Nature's grace is astoundingly generative. For all the trees we've ransacked, they still pump out endless supplies of oxygen. For all our careless light pollution, somehow Orion still shines down upon Brooklyn rooftops on late summer nights. For all the fireworks we set off that scare the living daylights out of our favorite birds, they return to our feeders the next morning—disoriented, but dutiful. And as much agency and comfort and naturalness that we've manipulated out of dogs, they sit by our sides, calm and caring, still ready to chase a predator away from the tribe.

I lie awake at night thinking about how they're still building even bigger cruise ships in the midst of our climate crisis and I get so stressed out. I hear about a trendy new dog breed and I want to scream out loud on the subway. I don't know how I'm going to get to bed after seeing the top-ten celebrities' carbon emissions. Oh, how much insomnia is caused when not every individual on the planet completely agrees with you!

So I have to find a way to reconcile this all somehow, if only to get at least a few hours of sleep.

A species like humans with such big hearts and brains, plus unlimited power over the natural world, is inevitably going to flail around and make all kinds of mistakes that seem beyond atonement. And maybe we are. Maybe there's no going back from the mess we made out of wolves. Can we ever be forgiven for creating an animal that we only selectively care for?

I have to believe we can. But it's going to require that we look far beyond our own impulses. We can't keep spoiling only the animals that make us feel good about ourselves, but we must care about the ones that may challenge our egos because they don't look and behave exactly as we would wish.

A first step: If you own a dog, let them inspire you. Look into their big adoring eyes and see the eyes of other creatures in them— elk, bison, mice, or the spider who didn't mean to wander into your sink.

Climate writer Nathanael Johnson articulates this hope so beautifully: "When you are able to affix yourself somehow, to bridge the abyss with a relationship with another creature of any sort, it's easier to make the case that there is some way in which the whole of creation matters, that it has, if not a purpose, at least an invigorating vitality."

This was my own *Matrix* red-pill journey once I fell head over heels in love with my small, sensitive shelter cat. If she had such a distinct personality, with specific opinions and fears and desires that didn't match in cookie-cutter lineup with other cats I had known, then surely each cow and each duck and each rat had their own personalities and their own value as well. Once I awoke to the preciousness of one animal, and to her suffering, I couldn't unsee the preciousness and potential suffering of all animals. And, subsequently, their home—our precious and suffering planet.

I wish our relationship with naturally evolving wolves had been more than enough to inspire future civilizations to see worth in all the varied lives on earth, but it's not too late. We can still learn great lessons from the round-headed descendants of wild canines, who love us in spite of our transgressions. Let's accept that grace as a call to love better and do better for all living things in our midst, who are still on our side.

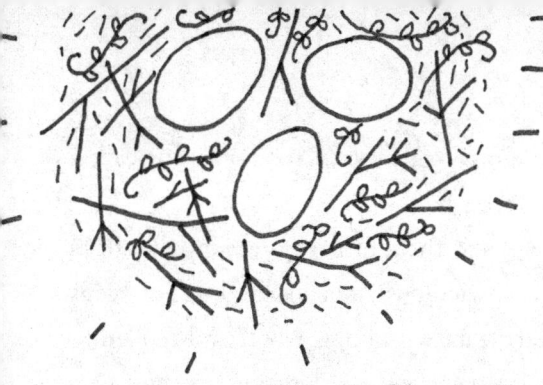

Chapter 17

ON MOURNING DOVES
AND TRYING AGAIN

February 26, 2020, was Ash Wednesday. By then, there were over 2,700 deaths worldwide.

I got ashes spread across my forehead: "You are from dust, and to dust you will return."

The first part, I can deal with. I am from stardust, moonlight, impermanence. From dust, this world emerged. But I want to be as permanent as I feel. "To dust you will return." No, thank you. It's distressing to think about the return.

Three months later, I peered out onto my East Village fire-escape balcony, distracted by the chaos of early summer growth: trees wildly filling out and crowding one another. *Opposite of social distancing*, I thought with a smile.

In the middle of all of it, a dead plant on my balcony. It would have been easy enough to dispose of it but then it would be easy to do a lot of things that I never get around to doing. Instead, I thought *UGH!* every time I saw it.

A couple of weeks later, I saw three little eggs among the sticks of the dead plant. A nest, meticulously constructed out of twigs and fabric scraps! My heart leapt with hope. My friend replied to my photo, saying that the doves chose my balcony for their nest because they knew I'd see meaning in it.

But what meaning? "Life in the midst of death" was too cliché, so I searched for another interpretation.

I decided for the time being that the signs of life in the dead plant were speaking to communal living: not everything is about me. The apartment I really wanted went to someone who surely wanted it just as much as I did. The rain that interfered with my walk was nourishing a dying tree. A plant of no use to me was now home and life for a bird family.

I considered the beauty of not getting my way.

The little bird home began to serve as an emotional harbor for me. My heart had started numbing to the accounts of death numbers—too abstract for a human mind to take in—but when I saw three perfect eggs, three little jewels, laid lovingly in the rag-tag nest, I could feel the *thump-thump* once again. *Life!*

I consider: "To everything there is a season, and a time for every purpose."

I remember a scene from the movie *The Secret Garden*:

"It's dead, anyhow."

"This garden's not dead. . . . There'll be so many roses in here this summer, you'll be sick of them."

On the tenth day of my daily egg watch, I noticed that while there had been three eggs, now there was only one. My stomach flopped, and I scanned around my balcony—had they rolled off?

Then, just to the side of the nest, I saw the two cracked eggs: empty spotted shells, partially shattered. Frantic, I searched the internet for what could have happened and learned that other animals and even other birds will steal eggs as a snack and leave the shells. I took the blame for the precariousness of my fire escape balcony—how could I have let it fail them?

Every sadness in 2020 was layered onto another sadness.

I spent the next morning at a large school gym, packing kits of groceries and household supplies for a food bank that would deliver them to elderly people in an affordable housing complex, a building they likely hadn't left since March. Their windows were tiny and smudged, little portals from a stuffy, cluttered apartment to a wide, empty city.

We stood four to six feet apart, counting cans of beans, batteries, cloth masks, and oranges to go in the bags. For an hour, my job was to staple together photocopied pages of crossword puzzles, word searches, coloring pages, and tips for handwashing with illustrations of a puppy using a sudsy bar of soap.

My heart broke, looking at some of the half-copied pages. What if someone wanted to finish the word search? What if they didn't have a TV, any books, and this would be the only distraction they got all day? What if they wanted to color the butterfly but couldn't go buy crayons because their immune system was too weak to take the elevator down fourteen floors and go to the drugstore? I heard that animal control had taken some of their pets. What if this puppy illustration made them ache with worry for the twelve-year-old mutt who was now in a lonely cage and likely wouldn't get adopted or reunited?

I had a few more minutes on my volunteer shift and snuck extra oranges into the remaining bags, hoping the sweetness could punctuate someone's long, boring, terrifying afternoon.

Afterward, hundreds of bags were lined up orderly and upright; all I could think about were the people in another building, somewhere, straining to see the sun, wishing for an orange.

I came back to my apartment ready to check on my little bird home. *Maybe some people who live in that building have their own bird friends*, I thought. But when I looked, the third egg was cracked open, the new life gone. "No," I whisper-prayed, and began crying, letting all the water of sorrow that had pooled behind my eyes fall out to the ground.

I opened my window and reached out to the nest, letting my hand hover above the shell as though I could summon it back into wholeness. I resisted touching it, though a part of me wanted to touch the sensation of despair, to hold death in my hands after months of avoiding any touch.

Death and fear had invaded my city for the past couple of months, but none of it was palpable. My friend's beloved mother died of Covid-19 early on; I sent ice cream via delivery because it felt dangerous to go to her doorstep. Without contact, we had no way to touch the sadness.

I wanted to crumble those eggshells in my fingers, crush them beneath my nails and wail for all that was lost: these little birds and a stranger in a yellow sweater whose obituary in today's paper stung my sternum. I never missed hugging people, I never missed restaurants; I missed people in yellow sweaters whom I'd never met, and all the summers they'd never get to have.

The summer rains started that afternoon, and they continued for three days.

The parent doves came back, looking confused. The dad walked around the nest, scanning and searching as I had. He sat for a few minutes on the nest, then flew away.

I googled "Do doves experience grief?" One author suggested that just as every human expresses grief differently, so do birds. Some have been known to "deny," their behavior completely unchanging. Others exhibit drooped postures in response to loss. Some will cry out, as though expecting a clarifying response from the dead companion.

In this particular family's case, both mother and father dove repeatedly searched around the nest in confusion. They peered into the cracked shells, then nuzzled them around a little.

It seemed like they were doing what we were all doing: searching in the midst of confusion. "Dust to dust." Nothing made sense. I scraped the bottoms of songs, nature, and history.

I grieved by nuzzling around shells.

I spent another day putting masks in plastic bags to hand out at the food bank, along with instructions on how to clean masks. Later that day, I read poems about World War II and realized how many of them were written over ten years after the war ended. I supposed that was how long it took for people to begin piecing scraps of feeling together. And still, it made no sense.

The doves flew away eventually, and didn't come back. I felt sick with guilt. Now what had I done wrong? I'd failed this family, who had worked so hard to bring new life to our city. I cried, and cried, and cried.

The nest disintegrated; how quickly it returned to a pile of sticks from a home. I resumed volunteer work, bringing prescription medication to people who couldn't leave their buildings. And the city adapted, offering to-go cocktails for the first time, which brought some jubilance to the bare humid streets.

People started to meet up outside, though I was still afraid for days after a friend hugged me before a park walk. Happiness felt limited and illicit, like it had to be seized and then quickly savored before it went away.

A jazz band playing while people danced on the sidewalk was almost more joy than I could bear, as though it exceeded our daily rations for beauty and delight. When the last song ended, the pavement quickly transformed from a dance floor back to a sidewalk.

One late summer evening, a couple of months after the eggs had been pecked to their demise, I saw a plastic neon-green straw resting on my balcony. I hadn't a clue how it would have gotten there; possibly a remnant from a to-go cocktail swept up the fire escape stairs.

But over the next day, I watched the same pair of mourning doves add twigs, and more straws, and pieces of lint or cigarette butts or receipt paper to the balcony. They were at it again. They were creating another nest for another shot at new life.

There is no doubt that animals grieve as we do, but they regulate stress through their bodies much more expertly than we do. Watch a cat return home from the vet, or a bunny who has just escaped a fox hunt. They vigorously shake to release tension, quite literally shaking off the trauma, and then go about their day. They don't let the event stick in bodies for lifelong storage the way humans do. They could stop trying after failure but instead they shimmy out the hurt and then give it another go.

Living things are built to adapt; in fact, we very much want to. Our bodies heal without us even trying; we grow without meaning to. We are evolved and designed for it—we can't survive if we don't, somehow, keep going.

Throughout the creation of the new nest, I thought of this line from a Jan Richardson poem: "The heart's sole remedy / for breaking / is to love still."

I can never understand why the mourning doves would return to the same place where they watched their babies die one by one to try again, but I suppose it is exactly that: The mystery of how a heart so broken can go on beating as if it were made precisely for this. The mystery of how a dove pair in their grief could go on nesting as though they were made precisely for this.

I'm reminded of caterpillars in a chrysalis, that favorite image of transitional growing pains, before emerging as a bright-blue butterfly. During the time inside the cocoon, the caterpillar begins breaking down as though it were dying. It thinks it is dying. And then one day, it has wings. How's that for a metaphor.

Life is rarely that tidy. New York City didn't grow new wings after the pandemic. Hardship doesn't always make us stronger. On the contrary, in many ways we are weaker for it. The ripple effects cut friend groups in half, jacked up rent, disrupted school enrollment, strained health services, closed beloved businesses, and devastated people's livelihoods.

Most of us weren't the strong, resilient butterflies, ripping off our masks and skipping into a citywide celebration. We weren't mourning doves building new nests.

Humans are not able to shake off our trauma; it burrows into our body and emerges when we least expect it—glancing at a magazine at the grocery store or grabbing onto a scent that we thought belonged only to one person.

I can't provide a tidy conclusion about my dove family; I moved from my apartment to Brooklyn before I knew whether the eggs made it.

But I never forgot their reverence toward the sacred Maybe, a word that has saved generations from the threat of Never. Maybe this egg. Maybe this time. Maybe this one. Maybe this date. Maybe this year. Maybe this job. Maybe God, maybe eternity, maybe miracles. Maybe life after death. Maybe emergence from dust.

Whenever I return to the East Village and see the mourning doves that fly from fire escape to fire escape, I look at each one like she's a miracle of the Maybe. And I think, *Maybe I too can try again*.

And all Manner of Things Shall Be Well......

Chapter 18

ON HUMANS
AND BEING A
LIVING THING

Death came to Norwich in the summer of 1349.

The English city shimmered on those warm days, the way that any city made of stone shines when the sun brightens gray walls and damp cobblestones.

Julian was going to turn seven years old that fall. The city's cathedral spire was eighty-four times her height; the city was not constructed for little girls but for national dominance. Norwich was the largest and wealthiest provincial city in England, a trading hub and center of power.

Even so, Julian found her way through the city, following the stray cats through the alleys and sneaking hot pretzels from market carts. She skipped past the libraries into the meadow and found cool refuge under the blackthorn tree, counting ladybugs and creating homes for fairies out of sticks and pebbles. She had a gift for finding sweet tenderness in the overwhelming city around her.

In a couple of days, she'd get to stay up late for an evening feast to celebrate Midsummer. She'd watch the older girls flirt and dance with unmarried men, the only opportunity they had to do so without the scornful eyes of priests. It was a time when even adults believed in fairies, and everyone indulged in magic. Rowdy teenage boys jumped through fires and rolled hay bales aflame down the hills to predict the luck of the harvest season and to express the glorious freedom of a drunken musical solstice night. Julian ran barefoot, weaving in and out of dances circling bonfires, the flames promising to ward off evil.

A few weeks after that celebration of life and abundance, a couple of tradesmen in town got very sick, very fast. They noticed painful, bloody swelling in their groins or armpits, then days of constant hacking of infected phlegm, then sudden death. The pattern repeated itself with neighbors: a sore armpit soon turned to misery soon turned to death, all thanks to a gravely mysterious illness.

The plague.

The disease slithered up Europe from the south, brought in on boats by French sailors and spread by fleas. Norwich had gotten news that towns were overwhelmed by plague, so it closed its city gates to ward off the disease, not knowing it was already thriving within its walls.

Within months, Julian saw the richest men in town fall to their deaths in the same alley where beggars had been lying dead for days. The harvest that townspeople prayed for during the Midsummer festival erupted in abundance, but there were few people to appreciate it. In nearby fields, dairy cows cried in discomfort with no one to milk them, and unharvested crops lay rotting.

Julian used to wake up to the sound of market carts creaking through the streets at dawn; now two thirds of the market stalls were empty, and a different cart rolled through the streets: "Bring out your dead!" the body collector cried, clanging a bell. A culture dependent on ritual for meaning had no choice but to unceremoniously discard its children, grandparents, friends, and leaders into a pile of bodies on a cart.

Julian, who was meticulously taught the liturgies, rituals, and mandates of the Catholic Church, couldn't make sense of why they no longer applied. Her only structured sense of the world had changed in an instant.

In two years, half the city had died.

From that point on, death was Julian's companion; it marked her childhood as much as French lessons, wooden dolls, and nightmares in her little bed. For twenty-one more years, aggressive outbreaks flared up in the east of England. It's likely that as an adult, Julian lost her husband and children to the Black Plague, and no doubt many mentors, companions, and beloved neighbors, like the man who sold her bread and the friendly groundskeeper of the local church who used to give her sweets as a child.

She witnessed a powerful city cower in illness, brought to its knees by terror. She witnessed educated men grapple to make sense of what was happening. Some believed the disease spread through imagination: simply thinking about it could summon it into the home. Others relied on scapegoats: it was heretics, it was the Jews.

Julian watched as enormous groups of men walked village to

village, flagellating themselves in an effort to win God's pardon by punishing themselves for collective sin.

Humans were bad, and God was angry, so nature was attacking them.

Julian's early childhood of wonder felt like a distant dream. She had avoided catching the disease that had taken so many loved ones away from her, but after decades of trauma she experienced a different kind of illness: profound heartache.

On what she thought was her deathbed at age thirty, Julian most likely suffered some kind of mental breakdown: How much more could she take? Did she really live in a universe so angry that it would steal children from the shade of blackthorn trees? Did the Creator hate this world he created?

In the midst of these moments, everything changed. Julian had a series of visions encouraging her to turn to the Creator not as a punishing father but as a loving mother.

From her bed over the course of several hours, she feverishly scribbled down the revelations that came to her during the loneliest and darkest hours of her life. While she thought she was dying, Julian survived the night and felt called to share all that she'd experienced during her hellish mental journey.

During Julian's time, men regarded women as "natural" because their ability to bear children would never allow them to mentally transcend their bodies the way that men could. Men dismissed their own natural bodies as they prioritized the mind, but they concluded that women were biologically unable to do so and therefore were part of Creation. That meant men had dominion over them.

Julian insisted on the divine feminine and stood up for the

wonder and beauty of our bodies, what she called "this beautiful human nature out of which we all arise." She referred to the union of body and soul as "a glorious union," not something to be transcended or dismissed.

In contrast to the self-hating despair aroused by much of Western religion of the era, Julian taught time and time again that the first goodness is the goodness of nature, and we are part of nature—not above or below it.

Despite the odds against her—a life filled with death and a society built on fear and despair—Julian believed in a benevolent universe. She stood up to the folly of people blaming nature for the plague or humans for being bad. Others cast fear and blame and ran away from nature. Her response was utterly different: creation was synonymous with goodness and love.

"All shall be well," she famously said. "All shall be well, and all manner of things shall be well."

This isn't Julian doing her best Pollyanna impression. She's referring to an earth that we are a small part of, a good earth whether events unfold according to our hoped-for outcomes or not.

Julian believed there was no separation between nature and humans; we were all part of it, equally dependent on one another, as deeply interconnected with the hazelnuts as much as with our fellow person. No human sin was to blame for the disease, she insisted, and went out of her way to assert that Jews were not responsible for the plague.

To Julian, claiming our natural state meant claiming our inherent goodness. As the flowers were made with great unconditional love, so were we, she concluded.

Having lived through three massive waves of the plague by the time she started writing, Julian is known for her radically optimistic philosophy. During her visions, she asked God point-blank to teach her about sin, and all she could see was love. I imagine her God to be a soft, floral-smelling grandmother who erupts in delight every time she sees you, who always has cookies waiting and a teakettle on, ready to hear your stories and soothe your troubles.

After decades of loss and excruciating mental pain, Julian fell in love with the world again the way we might fall back in love with a long-term companion: She focused on its small sweetness and endearing flaws. She wrote not from a place of ignoring reality but of deepening into it, confronting it with radical love.

For the powerful men of Julian's time to have admitted that we were a part of nature, every bit as much as grasshoppers and stallions, would've been to abandon the hierarchy that preserved their power.

Her society was a remnant of Rome, the imperial society that arranged nature into a hierarchal order, with women and other undesirables lumped with the animal world. Romans who studied such radical Indigenous societies like the Celts couldn't get over the fact that they worshipped without temples and viewed the feminine as sacred.

The empire did not want to be told that rivers and butterflies and women were sacred, because then it could not do whatever it wished to them with impunity. Imperial religion was created to serve the empire and solidify doctrine that supported the idea that people and other naturally occurring phenomena are to be controlled and used rather than related to and revered. The sacredness of earth, much less the sacredness of every human being, was a challenge to the powerful.

Roman Catholicism during the empire accentuated the teaching of original sin, meaning that infants inherit a tainted nature with a need for repentance. Bummer, right? Even hundreds of years later in Julian's time, it shook the world to hear "You are inherently good. And, for that matter, so are enslaved people, and turtles, and the fields of wheat over the hills."

As naturalist Lyanda Lynn Haupt puts it, Julian of Norwich "innately apprehended the graced interconnection of life."

In our time, we still separate ourselves from the earth as though we're trying to prove that we're robots.

It's empire thinking.

Eco-philosopher Thomas Berry observed, "While we have more scientific knowledge of the universe than any people ever had, it is not the type of knowledge that leads to an intimate presence within a meaningful universe. . . . The difficulty is that with the rise of the modern sciences we began to think of the universe as a collection of objects rather than a communion of subjects."

We still define animals as beings that *we are not like* rather than explore our glorious and embarrassing similarities. Science so often betrays our animal nature rather than uplifts it as a privilege—or as a mere fact of crawling upon this fecund planet.

Rather than denying our animal-ness to the point of utter rejection, appreciating our creatureliness might help restore the common doctrine across Indigenous societies that all life is holy and every species is sacred. We can begin to unravel the empire's insistence that humanity is sinful and we should be ashamed of our naturalness. We can come back to an ancient inner knowing that the truth is not doled out by those in power but accessed from deep within by everyone.

I think, way down in the brain of my belly, that we have simply neglected our interrelationships. As little children we see the sacred essence of all things, but it works better for our society if we ignore it as adults. Maybe human nature is not instinctively greedy and selfish. Maybe human nature is actually reverent toward all things, and greed is in fact a denial of what is natural to us.

I want to live in awe and interconnectedness like Julian.

Because I've been trained for decades with the tools of the empire, this will take some work. How funny that I've become so distant from my own human creature that I have to study my napping cat in order to remember how I once breathed as a baby: slow and big, my tummy rising like a boule of sourdough with every inhale of the earth's life-force.

I watch my cat to remember how to be mortal. When sick, she retreats and rests, and glances up from her paw to see that I'm still there. She doesn't try to do anything else or be anything else; she is pure body, hurting and sleeping.

I observe a street dog and remember my animal-like curiosity, the way I want my nose to lead me toward interesting people and to sniff my way into conversations not meant for my ears. I want to try every sizzling street food and meet every person and go down every shadowy corner where I see others headed. This shaggy mutt has a heart bigger than a star; he wants nothing but his own experience of the world he was born into, behind the garbage can where he learned how to scavenge.

One cold, wet night in Brooklyn, my heart bruised and my hope dangling off a ledge, I saw a raccoon wobble down the sidewalk, as damp and funny looking as me beneath the orange streetlight. Another one scampered out and nudged him. That's when I realized the wobbler was limping. The faster one scurried to the wobbler's other side and guided him as he stumbled all the way back to the bushes.

That night, I teared up looking at the no-nonsense kindness, and I remembered how to be a living thing.

RESOURCES

CHAPTER 1

Marino, Lori. "Concrete Tanks Are Torture for Social, Intelligent Killer Whales" *Aeon*, February 2, 2021. aeon.co/essays/concrete-tanks-are-torture-for-social -intelligent-killer-whales.

Gungor, Michael, host. "I'll Be Happy If . . ." *The Liturgists Podcast.* Interview with Peter Rollins. April 30, 2020. open.spotify.com/episode/5rJE1Htpexme 3WVxfgnIKX.

Burkeman, Oliver. "Escaping the Efficiency Trap—and Finding Some Peace of Mind." *The Wall Street Journal*, 2021. wsj.com/articles/escaping-the-efficiency -trap-and-finding-some-peace-of-mind-11630960194.

CHAPTER 2

Will, George. "When the Gorilla Speaks." *The Washington Post*, January 31, 1985. washingtonpost.com/lifestyle/1985/01/31.

Patterson, Francine. *Koko's Kitten.* Illustrated and photographed by Ronald H. Cohn. Paperback ed. New York: Bantam Books, 1987.

CHAPTER 3

Johnson, Kimberly Ann. *Call of the Wild: How We Heal Trauma, Awaken Our Own Power, and Use It for Good.* Hardcover ed. New York: Harper Wave, 2021.

Foster, Charles. *Being a Human: Adventures in 40,000 Years of Consciousness.* Hardcover ed. London: Profile Books, 2021.

CHAPTER 4

McBride, Hillary L. *The Wisdom of Your Body.* Paperback ed. Toronto: Harper-Collins, 2021.

Radke, Heather. *Butts: A Backstory*. Paperback ed. New York: Avid Reader Press, 2023.

Schoenbrun, Jane, dir. *I Saw the TV Glow*. A24, 2024.

Finch, Jamie Lee. "Your Body Is a Person." Online course. Accessed January 17, 2024. course.jamieleefinch.com/pages/your-body-is-a-person.

CHAPTER 5

Meehl, Cindy, dir. *Buck*. IFC Films; AMC Plus Documentaries, 2011.

CHAPTER 6

Haraway, Donna J. *Staying with the Trouble: Making Kin in the Chthulucene*. Durham, NC: Duke University Press, 2016.

Lorde, Audre. "The Master's Tools Will Never Dismantle the Master's House." In *Sister Outsider: Essays and Speeches*, edited by Barbara Smith, 110–14. Berkeley, CA: Crossing Press, 2007.

Rosenberg, Marshall B. *Nonviolent Communication: A Language of Life*. Foreword by Deepak Chopra. 3rd ed. Encinitas, CA: PuddleDancer Press, 2015.

Stone, Douglas, Bruce Patton, and Sheila Heen. *Difficult Conversations: How to Discuss What Matters Most*. New York: Penguin Books, 2010.

Ripley, Amanda. *High Conflict: Why We Get Trapped and How We Get Out*. New York: Simon and Schuster, 2022.

CHAPTER 7

Irvine, Leslie. *My Dog Always Eats First: Homeless People and Their Animals*. Lynne Rienner Publishers, 2013.

Rosenthal, Tracy. "Inside LA's Homeless Industrial Complex." *The New Republic*, May 19, 2022. newrepublic.com/article/166383/los-angeles-echo-park -homeless-industrial-complex.

Bulger, Jay, and Paula Aceves. "In Line at St. Brigid: The City's Campaign to Push Migrants out Has Turned Their Lives into an Interminable Loop." *Curbed*, February 26, 2024. curbed.com/article/nyc-migrants-shelter-stories-st-brigid -church-reticketing.html.

CHAPTER 8

Black, Riley. *The Last Days of the Dinosaurs: An Asteroid, Extinction, and the Beginning of Our World*. Hardcover ed. New York: St. Martin's Press, 2022.

CHAPTER 10

Kingsolver, Barbara. *Small Wonder: Essays*. Paperback ed. New York: Harper Perennial, 2003.

Tippett, Krista, host. "Robin Wall Kimmerer: The Intelligence of Plants." *On Being*, February 25, 2016. Last updated May 12, 2022. onbeing.org/pro grams/robin-wall-kimmerer-the-intelligence-of-plants-2022.

CHAPTER 11

Robinson, Marilynne. *Gilead*. Paperback ed. New York: Picador, 2009.

Buechner, Frederick. *Whistling in the Dark: A Doubter's Dictionary*. Paperback ed. San Francisco: HarperSanFrancisco, 1993.

Buechner, Frederick. *Wishful Thinking: A Seeker's ABC*. Paperback ed. San Francisco: HarperSanFrancisco, 1993.

Birdwatcher's General Store. "How the Cardinal Got Its Name." Accessed January 17, 2025. birdwatchersgeneralstore.com/how-the-cardinal-got-its -name.

CHAPTER 12

Herzog, Hal. *Some We Love, Some We Hate, Some We Eat: Why It's So Hard to Think Straight About Animals*. 2nd ed. New York: Harper Perennial, 2021.

Brookshire, Bethany. *Pests: How Humans Create Animal Villains*. Hardcover ed. New York: Ecco, 2022.

Sullivan, Robert. *Rats: Observations on the History & Habitat of the City's Most Unwanted Inhabitants*. New York: Bloomsbury, 2005.

Freeman, Doreen Patricia. "A Theology of Disgust." PhD diss., University of Exeter, February 2010. ore.exeter.ac.uk/repository/bitstream/handle/10036/3367 /FreemanD.pdf.

MacKinnon, J. B. "In Defense of the Rat." *Sierra: The Magazine of the Sierra Club*. October 28, 2023. sierraclub.org/sierra/rats-and-why-to-love-them.

Bernstein Network. "Rats Play Hide and Seek." September 13, 2019. bernstein -network.de/en/newsroom/news/20190913.

CHAPTER 13

Amiguet, Marie, dir. *The Velvet Queen*. Madman Entertainment, 2022.

Drexler, Jorge. "Movimiento." Track 1 on *Salvavidas de hielo*. Produced by Carles Campón. Warner Music Spain. Released September 22, 2017.

Chapter 14

Wohlleben, Peter. *The Inner Life of Animals: Love, Grief, and Compassion—Surprising Observations of a Hidden World*. Translated by Jane Billinghurst. Hardcover ed. New York: Greystone Books, 2017.

Merrifield, Andy. *The Wisdom of Donkeys: Finding Tranquility in a Chaotic World*. Paperback ed. New York: Walker, 2010.

Chapter 15

Johnson, Nathanael. *Unseen City: The Majesty of Pigeons, the Discreet Charm of Snails & Other Wonders of the Urban Wilderness*. Hardcover ed. New York: Rodale, 2016.

Mosco, Rosemary. *A Pocket Guide to Pigeon Watching: Getting to Know the World's Most Misunderstood Bird*. Paperback ed. New York: Workman Publishing, 2021.

Chapter 16

Brandow, Michael. *A Matter of Breeding: A Biting History of Pedigree Dogs and How the Quest for Status Has Harmed Man's Best Friend*. Paperback ed. New York: Beacon, 2015.

Morell, Virginia. "How Wolf Became Dog." *Scientific American*, July 1, 2015. scientificamerican.com/article/how-wolf-became-dog.

Chapter 17

Haupt, Lyanda Lynn. *Rooted: Life at the Crossroads of Science, Nature, and Spirit*. Paperback ed. New York: Little, Brown, 2023.

Starr, Mirabai. *Julian of Norwich: The Showings; Uncovering the Face of the Feminine in Revelations of Divine Love*. Paperback ed. Foreword by Richard Rohr. Newburyport, MA: Red Wheel/Weiser, 2022.

Starr, Mirabai, and Matthew Fox. "Julian of Norwich: A Bold, Gentle Visionary on Living in a Time of Pandemic." Online course. Accessed December 1, 2020. https://theshiftnetwork.com/course/01JulianOfNorwich01_20.

Berry, Thomas. *The Great Work: Our Way into the Future*. Paperback ed. New York: Bell Tower, 2000.

Fox, Matthew. *Order of the Sacred Earth: An Intergenerational Vision of Love and Action*. Paperback ed. Rhinebeck, NY: Monkfish, 2018.

ACKNOWLEDGMENTS

Thank you to the brilliant minds and kind hearts at Penguin: Meg Leder, Isabelle Alexander, Claire Vaccaro, and Lynn Buckley—for your intelligent edits, artistic guidance, and cheerful emails. Your enthusiastic support for my voice and this odd project is the biggest privilege of my life. To my agent and dear friend, Cindy Uh, your lioness-like loyalty and protectiveness motivate me to be a stronger writer and more daring person.

To my family—Mama, Dan, and Sunny—I can't stand how much I love you. I'll never understand how lucky I am to have any of you. I will explode if I think about it too hard, so for now, thank you and I love you more than you can know. To my beloved friends, and to my community at Trinity Lower East Side Lutheran Church, I'm so proud to be yours.

To the organizations whose phenomenal work honors the sacredness of all animal life: Woodstock Farm Sanctuary, the donkey sanctuary at Trinity Retreat Center, Catskill Animal Sanctuary, Best Friends Animal Society, Prospect Park Zoo, City Wildlife, and the Wild Bird Fund.

And to the organizations whose extraordinary work honors the dignity of all human life: PAWS NY, Sacred Streets, the chaplaincy team at Lenox Hill Hospital, and Trinity's Services and Food for the Homeless.

Thank you all for shaping this book and the way I see this beautiful world.